Quiltmaking for Beginners

Quiltmaking for Beginners

A STITCH-BY-STITCH GUIDE TO HAND AND MACHINE TECHNIQUES

LYNN G. KOUGH

THE QUILT DIGEST PRESS
NTC/Contemporary Publishing Group

Library of Congress Cataloging-in-Publication Data

Kough, Lynn G.
    Quiltmaking for beginners : a stitch-by-stitch guide to hand and machine
techniques / Lynn G. Kough.
        p.   cm.
    Includes bibliographical references (p. 135).
    ISBN 0-8442-2083-3
    1. Patchwork—Patterns.   2. Appliqué—Patterns.   3. Quilting.   4. Machine
quilting.   I. Title.
TT835.K68   1999
    746.46—dc21   98-42706
                                                                        CIP

*For my dearest friends in quilting—
the Over-the-Edge Quilters:*

*Joy Bohanan
Janice Byrne
Barbara Caffrey
Alison Curran
Lynn Liebenow
Jean Markowitz*

*Their steadfast loyalty, support,
and encouragement are treasured
gifts—rare and wonderful.
Their vision, humor, and many
talents are a joy to share.*

Editorial and production direction by Anne Knudsen
Art direction by Kim Bartko
Pattern editing by Kandy Peterson
Book design by Hespenheide Design
Cover design by Monica Baziuk
Cover photograph by Sharon Hoogstraten
Drawings by Kandy Peterson
Quilt photography by Sharon Risedorph
Other photography by Sharon Hoogstraten
Manufacturing direction by Pat Martin

Published by The Quilt Digest Press
An imprint of NTC/Contemporary Publishing Group, Inc.
4255 West Touhy Avenue, Lincolnwood (Chicago), Illinois 60646-1975, U.S.A.
International Standard Book Number: 0-8442-2083-3
Printed in Hong Kong
00 01 02 03 04 05 WKT 19 18 17 16 15 14 13 12 11 10 9 8 7 6 5 4 3 2 1

Acknowledgments

My grateful thanks to:

The quiltmakers—friends, old and new—for giving graciously of their time and energy

The editors, for their clarity and patience

The manufacturers, for generously sharing their excellent products

Cherrywood Fabrics, Inc.

Classic Traditions

Hoffman Fabrics

Mission Valley Textiles, Inc.

P & B Textiles

Springs Industries

And special loving thanks to my family—Al, Anne, and Katherine—who now recognize the book-writing virus and have learned to make great chicken soup!

Contents

Introduction

Welcome to the wonderful world of quiltmaking. Quilts hold a special place in many hearts. They provide beauty and warmth in the lives of the makers as well as those who view and use them. I invite you to come along and learn the basics of quiltmaking. These skills will provide a foundation as you learn to create your own beautiful quilts.

Books and magazine articles offering vast amounts of information are now available to the beginning quiltmaker. This is wonderful—but often overwhelming. My intent is to provide the "ground zero" basics for all would-be quilters—those who want to stitch by hand and those who wish to use the sewing machine. These techniques are presented side by side so that you may compare and try either or both.

There are many ways to sew by hand or machine. Each method is slightly different. What you will find here are strategies I know to be successful after teaching them for many years. You may choose to modify them as you become more adept or as you learn more tips and techniques. Throughout the text, I will also direct you to other useful sources.

Not only will you find quilt construction information, but also methods for dealing with color choices and fabric selection. This is an area that often confounds new (and experienced) quilters. I hope to ease you into the joys of using color and the pleasures of selecting fabrics. We are so fortunate to have a wonderfully diverse array of fabrics from which to make our quilts. There is truly something for every taste and style.

Above all, I encourage you to maintain a sense of humor and balance. Making quilts is *fun*! I firmly believe that there are rules in this world that we all ought to abide by—stopping at red lights, for instance. However, while there are those who are more comfortable with absolute rules for quiltmaking, I do not subscribe to that practice. There are too many instances when a rule hinders rather than helps. Instead, you will find guidelines and suggestions, tested over time. I encourage you to use common sense, learn what works for you, and concentrate on the enjoyment that quilts will bring to your life. We are all individuals, with differing viewpoints and abilities. One of the most attractive features of quiltmaking is that it allows for all of our divergent selves. I know you will delight in finding your place in the world of quilts.

HOW TO USE THIS BOOK

This book is designed as a basic course in quiltmaking, showing hand and machine techniques side by side, and emphasizing the fundamentals that are the quiltmaker's technical foundation. It does not attempt to show you everything you ever wanted to know about quiltmaking; rather, it enumerates the key tools and procedures you need to know and use to begin constructing wonderful quilts. And, although I know many quilters prefer pictures to words, I urge you to spend some time with the text: I promise you it will be worth the effort!

Before you begin a quilt project, be sure to read the two sections that follow this introduction—Quiltmaking Terms and Quiltmaking Tools. These will help you to get started on the right foot, and you can then refer to these materials at any time as you work through the rest of this book. Chapter 1 is also essential. Here, I explain the basics of fabric and color selection—a most important step in making a quilt.

Chapters 2 and 3 discuss the making of piecework blocks, explaining how patterns are created and how to translate them from drawings into stitched pieces of cloth. In Chapter 4, you will find 10 piecing projects with step-by-step directions. Each teaches a new technique as well as a lesson on color and fabric selection. They are arranged in order of increasing challenge, but well within the reach of a beginning quilter. Choose to work through the section in sequence or turn immediately to the technique or pattern that is of interest to you.

Chapter 5 introduces appliqué quilts, providing information on several approaches to creating this style of quilt. Two different styles of appliqué projects include many techniques for you to practice.

The color lessons for both the piecework and the appliqué quilts present possibilities beyond the quilts shown. The projects are modest in size to encourage you. Far too many people attempt to make a large quilt as a first project, soon abandoning it and quilting altogether. I'm urging you to think small to accomplish more. And while the adage may seem tiresome, practice can make perfect (or at least a whole lot better). There is repetition in each project to allow for practicing specific skills.

Chapters 6 and 7 explain how quilt blocks are transformed into a complete quilt top using block settings, sashings, and borders. You will also learn how to prepare your quilt for quilting. Chapters 8 and 9 cover the basics of hand and machine quilting. Chapter 10 explains the final steps in finishing your quilts—binding and labeling.

The book concludes with two sampler quilt projects, pattern templates, a resource list, and a bibliography, organized by topic to enable you to find additional information on a particular aspect of quiltmaking. I hope you will find it useful.

Now, shall we begin?

QUILTMAKING TERMS

Every craft has its own descriptive language and quiltmaking is no different. Spend a few moments with this short list of terms and, in no time, you'll be fluent in basic *quilt-speak*!

Appliqué. Stitching shaped pieces of cloth onto a background cloth to create a design.

Backing. The third layer of a quilt; can be a single fabric or several fabrics joined together.

Batting. The filler layer between the quilt top and backing; compression of this layer by the quilting stitch creates the raised motifs on the quilt surface; usually made of cotton, polyester, or a mix of these, although wool and silk batts are also available.

Binding. The standard edge finish for a quilt, made from folded strips of bias or straight-cut fabric, tightly stitched over the raw edges of the quilt.

Block. A square containing a pieced geometric design or an appliqué design; these may be simple or elaborate, and often have colorful and descriptive names; many quilt designs are created by repeating or combining blocks.

Border. Lengths of fabric stitched around the outside edges of the quilt top; these may be plain, pieced, or appliquéd.

Fusible web. A product that allows appliqué shapes to be cut from fabrics without seam allowances and bonded in place on the background fabric.

Grain of fabric. The alignment of threads from which fabric is made; it should be considered when cutting shapes from the fabric. **Straight grain:** Threads running parallel to the selvage (or woven) edge of the fabric; this is the straightest and strongest direction of the fabric; there is little or no stretch. **Cross-grain:** Threads running perpendicular to the straight grain threads; they are less tightly woven, so the fabric stretches more. **Bias:** A 45° diagonal across the threads; fabric cut in this direction has a great deal of stretch.

One-patch. An overall design formed by repeating a single shape, such as a square or a hexagon.

Piecework. Creating a geometric pattern by sewing individually shaped pieces of cloth together into that pattern.

Point to point. Joining two pieces of cloth along a seam line from the ¼" (0.75cm) mark at one end to the ¼" (0.75cm) mark at the other, as opposed to stitching the seam from cut edge to cut edge.

Pressing. Using an iron to smooth fabrics before cutting out shapes (try to move the iron parallel to the selvage); using an iron to flatten seam allowances after sewing pieces together (with an up-and-down motion, rather than back-and-forth). Most seam allowances are pressed to one side, toward the darker fabric when possible. Occasionally seams are pressed open. **Steam pressing:** I like a small amount of steam, but I am careful not to distort the fabric when it is damp. **Front or reverse side:** Pressing the reverse allows you to check seams; pressing the front allows you to make certain that the seam is flat. A judicious use of both is probably best.

Quilting. Using a running stitch to hold several layers of cloth together: a top layer with a design (the quilt top), a filler layer (usually batting), and a bottom layer (backing).

Rotary cutter, ruler, and cutting mat. A thin, extremely sharp revolving blade, available on a variety of handles; used to cut fabric by running the blade parallel to the edge of a thick plastic ruler, which is used to measure the desired fabric size and shape. The rotary cutter can only be used on the surface of the cutting mat, which allows the blade to slice through the fabric and slightly into the mat without damaging the blade.

Sashing. Strips of fabric stitched between the blocks as they are being set.

Seam allowance. The amount of fabric allowed beyond the stitching line; when two pieces of cloth are sewn together, there must be something for the thread to hang onto(!)—this is the seam allowance; most pieced designs use ¼" (0.75cm); appliqué designs use ³⁄₁₆" (0.5cm) or less.

Set. The way in which the completed blocks are arranged to make the quilt top.

Stabilizer. A paper-like product placed under the background fabric to support it and prevent distortion when doing machine-stitched appliqué.

Template. The pattern for each shape of a pieced or appliquéd design.

Whole cloth. Decorative quilting on one large piece of fabric or several pieces of the same fabric joined together; there is no piecework or appliqué.

These are the terms you will use most frequently as you make your quilts. Soon they will simply become a part of your everyday quiltmaking vocabulary.

Don't shortchange yourself or make your quilting needlessly difficult. For the most part, you probably don't need an extravagant item (I'm still quilting with the 99-cent thimble I bought years ago). But the truth is that some products are better made than others and will facilitate your work.

QUILTMAKING TOOLS

The tools for quiltmaking can be as simple or as elaborate as you wish. It seems that every week a new gadget appears on the market and, as you progress, you will no doubt find some that work particularly well for you. As a beginner, you will need a few essentials.

Basic Tools for Both Hand and Machine Work

Light source. Ideally, you will have good natural light at your work space, as well as adequate artificial light. Excellent daylight spectrum fluorescent fixtures are available.

Scissors. Three different scissors will do most of your cutting tasks. **Shears:** Strong, sharp, and *comfortable* for cutting fabric; usually 8″ (20cm). **Utility scissors:** Strong, sharp, and comfortable for cutting template plastic, paper, stabilizers, batting, etc.; these will *not* be used for cutting fabric; usually 8″ (20cm). **Embroidery scissors:** Small, sharp right to the points, comfortable; used primarily for trimming and clipping appliqué seams; usually 4″ or 5″ (10cm or 12cm); protect these points in a case. Purchase the best scissors that you can afford— those with a reputation for retaining their sharp edges, made by a company known for good customer service.

Rotary cutter, ruler, and cutting mat. These tools, described under Quiltmaking Terms, allow you to cut a number of pattern pieces from your fabric very efficiently. Or you may cut the same shaped piece from several fabrics at the same time. The equipment requires care in both use and storage (as do any fine tools).

Threads. Purchase good quality threads for all aspects of your quiltmaking. **Piecework:** Use 100% cotton or cotton-wrapped polyester-core threads; do not use quilting thread for piecework. **Appliqué:** A thinner thread, often advisable to create an invisible hand appliqué stitch; embroidery-weight machine stitching thread works well; decorative or transparent threads are often used for machine appliqué. **Quilting:** Fine results are produced by 100% cotton or cotton-wrapped polyester-core threads; check to see whether the thread is intended for hand or machine stitching.

Pins. A pin is not just a pin anymore! **Piecework:** Long 1⅛″ (2.75cm), thin, sharp pins with small or flat heads hold pieces accurately; quilting pins are really not suitable. **Appliqué:** Many stitchers prefer shorter ¾″ (2cm), sharp pins with small or flat heads to hold appliqué pieces in place without getting in the way of the needle and thread; sometimes called *sequin pins*. **Quilting:** Long 1¼″ to 1½″ (3cm to 3.75cm), heavier pins with ball heads are strong enough to pin the three layers of the quilt together for basting. **Safety pins:** Often used to baste the quilt layers together for machine quilting; they must be small and sharp.

Tape measure. A sturdy, accurate tape measure is an important tool, especially useful when measuring for border application.

Chalk pencils. One of several types of marking tools, used in a number of ways; especially useful to transfer quilting designs onto the quilt top.

Tools for Hand Work

Needles. Sharps: Used for both piecing and appliqué. I recommend a no. 10 for piecing and a no. 12 for appliqué. If you want more needle to hold onto as you piece, consider a no. 10 milliner's, or straw, needle. Betweens: Used for quilting; they are shorter than sharps and easier to manipulate with the thimble. I recommend a no. 9 or no. 10. These are really small needles, and it will take a little time to become accustomed to using them. You're not clumsy—it's an acquired skill and well worth the effort!

Thimble. While you may wish to use a sewing thimble with a rounded top for piecing, you will need a different thimble for quilting. Again there are choices, but the two that have proved most successful for my students are a metal one, with a flat top and raised edge, or a leather one, most often a finger-sheath type.

Rulers. A transparent ruler, 2″ × 18″ (5cm × 45cm), with a clearly marked ¼″ (0.75cm) line along its length, or a Plexiglas square rod, called a "quilter's quarter," are useful to mark cutting lines.

Marking pencils. Used to draw around templates, transferring the seamlines or appliqué shapes onto the fabric. Pencils are available in a variety of colors. Select those you can clearly see on both light and dark fabrics. These lines do not need to be erased, but they should not show through onto the right side of the fabric or around the edge of the appliqué. Avoid #2 lead pencils, ballpoint pens, and permanent markers. *Tip*: Placing a piece of fine-grain sandpaper under the fabric helps the pencils do their job more easily.

Quilting hoop or frame. Used to hold the quilt layers taut while doing "rocker" stitch quilting. There are many varieties available. If you choose a wooden hoop, find one that has beveled edges and is at least 1″ (2.5cm) wide with a diameter of at least 14″ (35cm). That allows you to quilt a decent amount before you need to move the hoop. Frames are available in wood and plastic pipe.

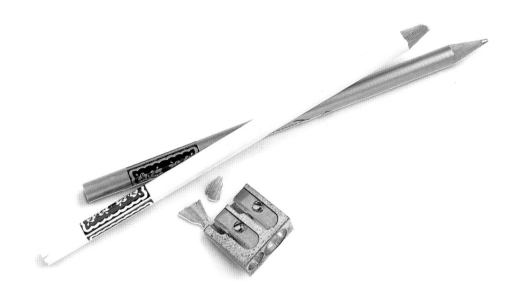

Tools for Machine Work

Sewing machine. All sewing machines are not created equal—not by a long shot! The quality of the machine is an important factor in the ease and enjoyment of your quiltmaking. If you do not own one with which you are comfortable, one that can sew a straight seam without pulling to the left or right, that makes consistently even stitches, has reliable tension, and that accepts different kinds of threads, think seriously about shopping around for a machine capable of performing these functions. If you wish to use your machine for piecework, appliqué, and quilting, you will want it to have several features: a straight stitch with adjustable length; a smooth, even satin stitch with adjustable width; a hemming stitch for invisible appliqué; the capacity to use the feet described here under "Machine presser feet"; and, if possible, a "needle-stop down" feature. Shop with a reputable dealer who gives lessons on how to use the machine and provides reliable service. Don't just look at the machine; test it! Sew on it and try the various functions that interest you. Many hours will be spent in the company of your sewing machine: choose a helpful partner, not a contentious combatant.

Machine needles. Use machine needles specific to certain quiltmaking tasks. A good, sharp needle can spell success. Frequently checking and changing the needle is the least expensive way to help the machine function at its best. Universal or jeans/denim (round-eye) needles are used for piecing. Long-eye (oval-eye) needles, such as topstitch, embroidery, quilting, and Metafil or Metallica, are used for specialty threads. The long-eye needle allows the specialty thread to pass through the needle and fabric with less drag and less breakage. Size 80/12 is most versatile. Use a larger size for thicker, decorative threads.

Machine presser feet. Specific feet greatly facilitate different parts of the quiltmaking process. **¼" (0.75cm) foot:** Designed to make sewing a ¼" seam more visible and accurate. **Open-toe foot:** May also be called an *embroidery foot*; allows you to see the edge of the appliqué and the placement of the machine stitching as you work. **Walking (even-feed) foot:** Works in tandem with the machine feed dogs and allows the quilt layers to pass evenly under this presser foot when doing machine quilting. **Darning (hopping) foot:** Used with the feed dogs disengaged to allow for free-motion machine quilting and embellishment.

Seam ripper. Look for a seam ripper with a fine, sharp tip and a sharp interior curve. Use this not just to "reverse" sew, but also to coax seams or difficult fabrics under the presser foot.

Chapter 1

Fabric and Color

Often, beginning quiltmakers find it difficult to make fabric and color selections. Yet these choices are at the very heart of your quilts, and, as experienced quilters will tell you, they can be a most enjoyable part of quiltmaking. The information here will save you time, money, and frustration as well as help you to develop your own personal style.

FABRIC SELECTION

Fabric is the "stuff" our quilt dreams are made of. The variety of available fabric is, depending on your viewpoint, either fabulous or overwhelming. It is wise to approach this wealth of choices in a logical, somewhat limited fashion. As a beginner, you will want to *choose fabric that works with you.* That means to select good-quality 100% cotton broadcloth (smooth, plain-weave, medium-weight cloth) or pima cotton (fine, tightly woven cloth).

Making a quilt requires time and effort on your part, both of which are valuable. Poor-quality cloth will make your work much more difficult and result in a disappointing product. Avoid heavily finished fabrics (which will feel stiff) and loosely woven fabrics (you can almost see through these when they are held up to the light). Be cautious about "bargain" fabric.

Focus fabric with value-graded
supporting fabrics

FABRIC PREPARATION

Preparation of the fabrics before you begin to sew is the next consideration. If the quilt is going to be washed at any time, you need to know that all of the fabrics can stand up to that treatment. No color from one fabric should bleed into another fabric. Neither should one fabric shrink a great deal. Today's fabrics are usually dye-fast and stable, but precaution is wise. You can choose to

- ◆ Wash (in a mild soap; no harsh detergents, please!) and dry the fabrics in the same way that the quilt will be treated
- ◆ Rinse and dry the fabrics
- ◆ Do nothing to the fabrics *except* test a swatch of each for shrinkage and color-fastness.

If a fabric bleeds, set the dye by soaking the cloth in undiluted white vinegar and rinsing thoroughly in cool water. If it continues to bleed, the best solution is to use a different fabric. Preshrink any questionable fabric. Avoid "beating up" your fabric and making it look old and used before you have begun. If you have washed or rinsed your fabrics, press them before cutting out the pattern pieces. Don't press until you are ready to use the fabric, as you will no doubt have to fold it to store it. Why do the same job twice?

COLOR CHOICE

Approach the selection of colors for your quilt as a trip to your favorite place. This is fun! Remembering that it is a physiological fact that we all see colors differently, *choose colors that please you*. Rely on your own instinct to select one color or to assemble a grouping of colors, or utilize combinations of colors, called *harmonies*, to create your color scheme.

Become familiar with the following short list of terms relating to color. The principles they define can aid you in selecting color combinations that make distinctive patterns in your quilts.

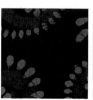

Hue

Tint

Shade

Tone

Describing Colors

Hue. The name of a color (red, orange, rose, peach, etc.)

Tint. Pure color mixed with white (pink, lavender, mint green, etc.)

Shade. Pure color mixed with black (eggplant, navy, etc.)

Tone. Pure color mixed with gray; these colors are dulled, have weak chroma

Chroma. The intensity, purity, or saturation of a color; strong chroma equals brilliant, vivid colors containing no black, white, or gray

Value. The *relative* lightness or darkness of a color

dark

medium

light

Value

The same floral fabric appears dark, medium, and light relative to the other fabrics.

Organizing Colors

Color circle or wheel. Colors organized in a circular sequence based on the spectrum; the primary colors on the most familiar circles are red, yellow, and blue.

In this color wheel, the largest wedges represent primary colors; the medium-sized wedges, secondary colors; and the smallest wedges, tertiary colors.

Harmonies. Combinations of color based on their position on the color wheel or simply on color itself.

Harmonies based on color are:
  Achromatic—black, white, and gray (or no color)
  Monochromatic—one color
  Polychromatic—many colors

Achromatic   Monochromatic   Polychromatic

Harmonies based on the color wheel are:
  Analogous—colors touching each other in one part of the color wheel and occupying less than half of the circle, using a minimum of three colors, a maximum of five

hot colors   cool colors
Analogous   Analogous

Complementary—colors located directly across the circle from each other
Split complementary—using a color with the two colors on either side of its complement (the complement is not used)
Double complementary—using two adjoining colors, plus both of their complements
Triadic—using three colors spaced at equal intervals around the wheel

yellow

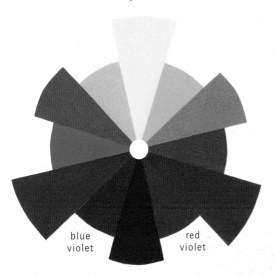

blue violet   red violet

Split Complimentary

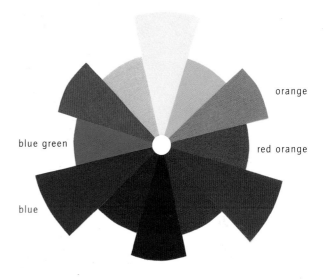

orange

blue green   red orange

blue

Double Complimentary

Don't try to grasp all of this at once. The more you use it, the more comfortable you will become. See how the words come to life in the project illustrations and samples. You will begin to appreciate how even a small understanding of color concepts will allow you to select more varied fabrics and create many interesting quilts. Consult the Bibliography for more in-depth color sources when you are ready.

red and green

blue and red

violet and yellow

Complementary

Contrast

In addition to selecting fabrics by content and color, we need to consider *value* and *pattern scale*. The design of the quilt is visible because of *contrasts* that appear in:

◆ color
◆ value of colors
◆ scale of patterned fabric

Colors that are close to each other on the color wheel offer little contrast. Choosing colors farther apart on the wheel creates more contrast.

Light colors used with dark colors will make a sharp demarcation in the quilt pattern. Using all light-value fabrics or all medium-value fabrics (a common problem for quilters) will result in little or no visible pattern. But remember that *value is always relative*: a particular fabric's value depends on the value of the surrounding fabrics.

Choosing fabrics for your quilt should include consideration of the *pattern type* (floral, geometric, novelty) and the *pattern scale* (size). For example, a group of fabrics that all have small floral patterns will cause the quilt design to become indistinct. Varying the type and scale of patterns allows for contrast. Mixing patterned and solid fabrics also provides design definition.

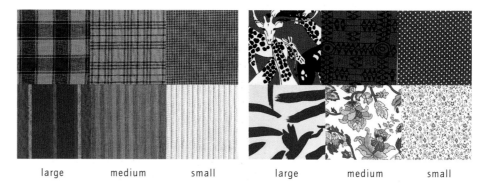

large   medium   small   large   medium   small

Pattern scale   Pattern scale

High contrast in each fabric created by color or value

Think about these ideas, and apply one concept at a time. Before you know it, you'll automatically consider color, value, pattern type, and scale as you select fabrics for your quilt projects. The selection process will become a wonderful treasure hunt!

Chapter 2

Understanding Piecework Blocks

This chapter explains how piecework blocks are formed and leads you through the techniques essential for making them. Reading this chapter before you begin a project will help you understand how that pattern is put together and transformed into fabric. As you become more experienced, the information here will help you tackle any geometric design with confidence.

HOW GEOMETRIC BLOCKS ARE FORMED

Traditional geometric block designs are formed by connecting points on a grid. The grid is created from a regular division of the total block area (fig. 2.1). This grid—or framework—provides the beginning and ending points for the lines that form the block's design. To figure the size of the pattern pieces, or *templates*, needed to create the block design in fabric, we need to know the desired size of the finished block. The underlying grid tells us how to divide that measurement. For an *Ohio Star* block (fig. 2.2), the grid tells us the measurement for each section of the block, based on the size of the entire block:

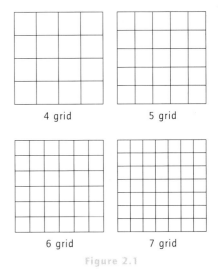

4 grid   5 grid

6 grid   7 grid

Figure 2.1

length of side divided by number of grid sections
= length of each grid section

The process remains the same for any block size and any grid division.

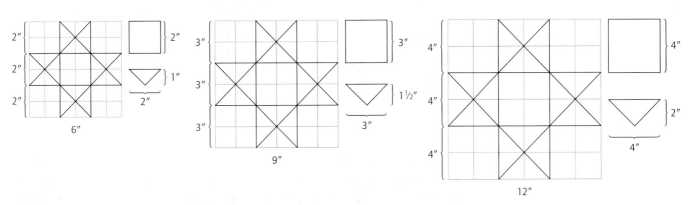

Figure 2.2

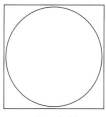

Too tight

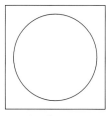

Ample space

Figure 2.3

Blocks Formed from Circles

Some block patterns are formed from circles. In this book you will meet three:

♦ *Chrysanthemum* (*Dresden Plate*)—based on a full circle
♦ *Fan*—based on a quarter circle
♦ *Drunkard's Path*—based on a quarter circle

Patterns can be made simply by selecting a finished block size and tracing a circular object (such as a plate) that fits within that square. Allow ample space around the circle for the background block (fig. 2.3). You may divide the circle into even-numbered sections by *accurately* folding a paper template into sections.

If you are more at home with a compass and protractor, you can construct the circle and its divisions (both even- and odd-numbered) using these tools. For example, the sixteen-petal chrysanthemum has individual petals based on dividing the circle into sixteen equal pieces (fig. 2.4). The circle = 360°; each petal = 22.5°:

$$360° ÷ 16 = 22.5°$$

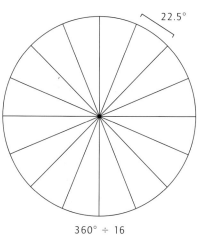

$360° ÷ 16$

Figure 2.4

TEMPLATES

Once you know the finished size of a template, you can make it. Templates for a hand-pieced project will be exactly the same size as the finished shapes. This allows you to trace the actual seamlines of each piece onto your fabric (fig. 2.5a). Seam allowance is added *after* this step. Templates for a machine-pieced project include ¼" (0.75 cm) around the design shapes (fig. 2.5b). Rather than following the line, as you do with hand stitching, use the presser foot to follow the cut edge of the fabric piece, with the machine needle aligned to stitch ¼" (0.75cm) from that edge.

Hand piecing   Machine piecing

   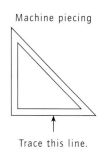

Trace this line.   Trace this line.

Figure 2.5a   Figure 2.5b

Making Templates

Templates can be made from flexible plastic, cardboard, paper, Plexiglas (thick plastic), and metal. Plexiglas or metal templates are commercially available in a variety of shapes and styles. Cardboard and paper can be used, but with utmost care, as they can change shape during use.

Different styles of template include:

◆ transparent or see-through, enabling you to feature different parts of the fabric motif, if you so desire, when you cut a shape
◆ opaque (not see-through)
◆ window or open in the center, most frequently made from metal

Remember, when making *hand-piecing* templates, cut just the pattern shape; when making *machine-piecing* templates, cut the pattern shape *plus* seam allowance. I recommend that you begin with good-quality, four-squares-to-the-inch (four-squares-to-the-cm) graph paper. Measure across the length and width. Unless both directions are correct, you cannot draw accurate templates.

1. Draw the shape you need onto the graph paper, following the printed lines. If this is a template for hand piecing, place a sheet of transparent, flexible template plastic over the shape and trace it onto the plastic.

2. For machine-piecing templates, use a thin transparent plastic ruler, such as a C-THRU® ruler, with an accurate ¼″ (0.75cm) grid to add seam allowance. Place the ¼″ (0.75cm) ruler line on the shape lines and draw along the edge of the ruler on the paper. Placing the transparent, flexible template plastic over the shape, trace the cutting (outside) lines onto the plastic.

3. To cut out these templates, I use a method I learned from Patricia Morris, well-known quilting teacher. You have probably always cut around a shape, holding that shape as you cut. With Pat's method you do the reverse. This moves the line to be cut *between* your eyes and the scissors blade (fig. 2.6a), instead of keeping the line *behind* the blade (fig. 2.6b). *Hold the part to be cut away* from the template shape, *instead of the shape itself.* Watch the scissor blades just shave away the line of the seam allowance or the seamline, depending on what type of template you are making. Therefore, when you draw or cut around this template, the pencil or the rotary blade is re-creating the placement of that line, not adding more to the size. Try it!

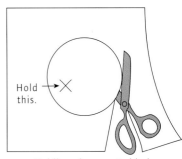

Holding shape puts blade between eyes and line.

Figure 2.6a

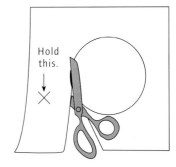

Holding background puts line between eyes and blade.

Figure 2.6b

ROTARY CUTTING

Rotary cutters are available in many forms. Olfa® and Fiskars® are respected brand names and represent the two most common handle types. I strongly recommend that you test before you buy. It is important that your hand is comfortable when you cut.

The most basic setup includes a cutter and mat—17″ × 23″ (45cm × 60cm) is the most versatile size—and at least one thick Plexiglas straight ruler. The ruler most often used to measure strips cut from lengths of fabric measures 6″ × 24″ (15cm × 60cm), allowing you to fold fabric in half, selvage to selvage, and cut strips across the fabric width. To recut these strips into smaller shapes, a smaller ruler is easier to handle. Sizes such as 4″ × 14″ (10cm × 35cm) and 6″ × 12″ (15cm × 30cm) work well.

These straight rulers are marked in inch increments, subdivided into ⅛″ (centimeter increments, subdivided into 0.25). Choose a ruler with clear markings, visible against both light and dark fabrics. Those with fewer lines can compromise the cutting process because you simply can't measure accurately. The ruler should also have several angles marked—45°, 60°, and 30° are helpful. These angles facilitate cutting bias binding, mitering corners, and cutting various triangle shapes.

Additional rulers are available in a multitude of shapes and sizes. The most useful ones help you to cut triangles and large squares. As your rotary skills grow and your quilt repertoire increases, you may wish to acquire more specific-to-task rulers.

You can also purchase sets of plastic template shapes grouped by size and/or specific quilt pattern (such as *Double Wedding Ring*). These are limited in scope and usefulness, but can be just the ticket for the right project.

A word about cutting mats. It is my experience that the smooth mats will not dull your rotary cutter blade as quickly as the pebbled ones. Not all line markings on the mats are accurate, so be careful. My preference over time has become the Omnimat® by Omnigrid®, which is green and accurately ruled on one side and reverses to a plain gray side.

Chapter 3

Piecework Techniques

As you select from Projects 1 to 10 in *Quiltmaking for Beginners*, refer to the information in this chapter. It is a good idea to read through carefully before you begin each new quilt, both as a refresher on those techniques you have used before and as an introduction to those you have not.

Whether you choose hand or machine methods—or a combination—before you begin cutting fabric, make sure you understand about grainline and can easily identify the straight grain of fabric (see page viii). Try to cut pieces so that the straight grain is on the outside edge of a unit or the block (fig. 3.1). This helps to keep seams from stretching. There are times, however, when the fabric design or the shape of the template dictates otherwise. Don't obsess about it; just remember grainline placement as a general rule of thumb. It is another technique that will enhance your quiltmaking and add to your enjoyment.

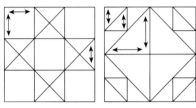

Straight of grain or cross-grain placement.

Figure 3.1

ACCURACY COUNTS

As you have discovered by now, quiltmaking is no different from lots of other things in this world—there is more than one way to do just about everything. The most important aspect, regardless of your method, is to be as scrupulously *accurate* as you can manage. The only way to achieve consistency in your blocks is to maintain accuracy in:

- ◆ template making
- ◆ cutting
- ◆ sewing

You must work repeatedly with the (almost legendary) ¼″ (0.75cm) seam. Try not to allow this to intimidate you. If you have never done any other sewing, it probably won't seem unusual. If you are used to garment sewing, it may take a while to adjust to using a smaller seam. Don't be discouraged. The more you sew, the easier it will become to stitch an accurate ¼″ (0.75cm) seam. Fabric is a wonderfully flexible and forgiving medium—you will learn how to work within its limits and your own to form a partnership.

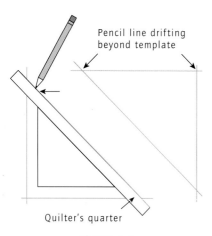

Pencil line drifting beyond template

Quilter's quarter

Figure 3.2

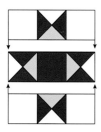

Figure 3.3a

Figure 3.3b

A word about pressing is in order here. It is too easy to press creases into your work or to stretch shape edges. The iron can be your best friend or worst enemy. It must be used prudently. Most often I rely on careful finger pressing and pinning when constructing individual units or blocks. Once the block is together, I press seams in place.

HAND WORK BASICS

1. Draw and cut out the templates, using utility scissors.
2. Prepare your fabrics. Press smooth.
3. Position the template on the *reverse* side of the fabric, keeping in mind the grainline. With a fabric-marking pencil, trace around each template. This is the seamline. When drawing seamlines, allow the pencil to drift just beyond the end of the template. It's difficult to mark exactly where the seam begins and ends. When the pencil drifts, it will cross the other seamline and give you a clear beginning and ending. Remember to leave enough room between traced shapes to add seam allowances. Using a quilter's quarter or transparent ruler, add a ¼" (0.75cm) seam allowance line around each shape (fig. 3.2). This is the cutting line. (Did you use a piece of fine-grain sandpaper under your fabric?)
4. Cut out the pieces with fabric shears. Keep similar pieces pinned together with a label or in a labeled plastic bag.
5. Select the sewing thread and needle. Use of a thimble is optional here. Sew the blocks together in units, following a piecing diagram when available. For example, the *Ohio Star* block contains five single squares and four units made of four triangles each. Stitch the triangle units first; join these and the squares into rows; join the rows together (fig. 3.3a). Most grid-based blocks will join with horizontal, vertical, or diagonal rows (fig. 3.3b). Remember, you are always sewing only one seam, or two fabric pieces together, only a single seam at a time, from point to point (fig. 3.4). It is handy to have a small flannel board on which to lay out the block pieces in order. Then you can pick up the pieces as you stitch and return them to their proper location.
6. To sew a seam, pick up two pieces of fabric and place them right sides together, holding the seam to be stitched at the top. Place a sharp, thin pin through the two pieces at one end of the seamline, carefully matching both ends. Repeat at the other end. Place a third pin at the center of the seamline, perpendicular to the seamline (fig. 3.5). *Reverse the end at which you begin stitching if you are left-handed.*
7. Thread your needle with no more than 18" (45cm) of thread; any more will just get in the way, since most of these seams are between

Figure 3.4

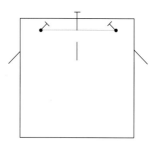

Figure 3.5

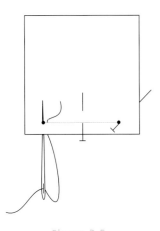

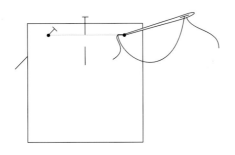

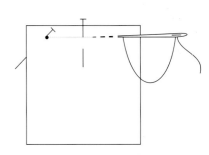

Figure 3.6   Figure 3.7   Figure 3.8

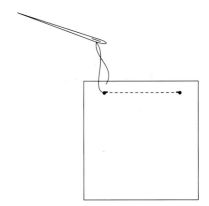

2″ and 6″ (5cm and 15cm) long. Use a single thread and put a small knot at one end. Turn the pieces to be stitched 180° in your hand. This puts the seam at the bottom. Insert the needle into the seamline just to the right of the left-end pin, pull the pin out, and bring the needle up through the pinhole at the end of the seam (fig. 3.6). Pull the thread through and take a small backstitch. Now return the seam to the top position, turning the pieces 180° in your hand. This puts your needle at the right end of the seam (fig. 3.7).

8. Make small running stitches, right to left, along the seamline, checking that you are stitching through both marked seamlines. Take a small backstitch every 8 or 10 stitches. You don't have to take each stitch separately as you go along the line. A running stitch usually means to load a number of stitches onto the needle before pulling the thread through (fig. 3.8). Often you get the sense of loading the fabric onto the needle, rather than pushing the needle through the fabric.

9. When you reach the other end point, pull the pin out, and bring the needle up through the pinhole. Make a small backstitch (fig. 3.9). Again rotate the pieces (the seam is now on the bottom). Take one stitch back along the seamline and knot the thread (fig 3.10). Clip the thread, leaving a ¼″ (0.75cm) tail. Keep your stitches pulled taut as you work, not tight enough to pucker the seam, but maintaining a firm seam.

10. Follow this procedure for a seamline that joins sewn units. Pin along the seamline, matching seams carefully. Remember, you are still only sewing two pieces together at a time, end point to end point. Stitch the first part of the seam as in Step 7, taking the backstitch in the first end point. Then pass the needle through the seam allowance to the next end point (fig. 3.11), making a backstitch there, and proceeding down the seamline. The joints should "snug up" close to each other since the two end points are separated only by two pieces of cloth. When you reach the last end point of this seam, finish the seam as in Step 9.

Figure 3.9

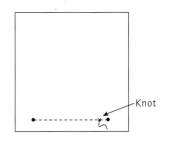

Figure 3.10

Knot

Figure 3.11

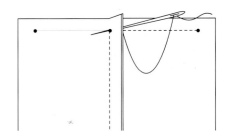

Selvages

Figure 3.12

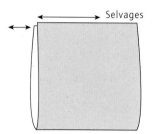

Selvages

Figure 3.13

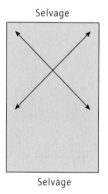

Selvage

Selvage

Figure 3.14

MACHINE WORK BASICS

1. Decide which shapes can be rotary cut and which require a template. Draw and cut out any templates.
2. Prepare your fabrics. Press smooth.
3. Place a cutting mat on the work surface with the short side of the mat near you. To straighten the end of the fabric from which you will cut a strip, fold the fabric in half, selvage to selvage, with right sides together (it is often easier to see the ruler lines against the wrong side of the fabric). It will probably "bubble" near the fold if you put the cut ends together (fig. 3.12).
4. Slide the selvage ends left to right against each other until the bubble disappears (fig. 3.13). Then lay the fabric on the mat, selvages toward you. If the cross-grain threads seem terribly crooked, pick up the fabric, and try gently stretching the piece on the bias from corner to corner (fig. 3.14). Then fold, realigning the selvages, get rid of any bubble, and place on your mat, with the right edge of the mat visible (fig. 3.15). *Reverse fabric and hand positions here and through Steps 5 and 6 if you are left-handed.*
5. Place the long edge of a 6" × 24" (15cm × 60cm) ruler close to the right (cut) edge of the fabric, aligning a horizontal measurement line with the fabric fold (fig. 3.16). Make certain that all of the fabric's cut edge is beyond the right edge of the ruler. Place your left fingertips down on the ruler, about a third of the way up from the selvage edge, and press down. Release the rotary cutter blade cover and grasp the cutter in your right hand. Holding the blade against the ruler's right edge, push the blade down and forward through the fabric. Some quilters can hold the ruler steady for a cut across the entire piece of fabric. For many, that doesn't work. If you are like most, momentarily stop the blade's forward progress when you reach the place where your left hand is holding down the ruler. Without moving the ruler or lifting the cutter, "walk" your left thumb and fingers up another third of the distance to the fold. Press down with your fingers and continue

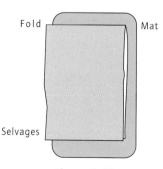

Fold   Mat

Selvages

Figure 3.15

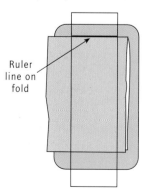

Ruler line on fold

Figure 3.16

pushing the rotary cutter forward. If necessary, do this step once
again.

6. Without lifting the fabric, rotate the mat and fabric 180°. This positions the fold of the fabric near you and the bulk of the fabric to your
"handedness." You can now easily measure and cut the strips needed
for your project (fig. 3.18). Most of these strips will be recut into
other shapes needed for your project. Since your machine needle is
guided by the cut edge of the fabric to sew the ¼" (0.75cm) seam,
accurate cutting is necessary. I do not recommend folding the fabric
into quarters to cut strips. It is entirely too easy for the resulting
strips to have wavy edges. Always restraighten the fabric edge perpendicular to the fold after cutting 6" to 8" (15cm to 20cm) from that
edge. Do it more often if you sneeze and your rotary cutter runs
amuck! Be patient. It takes some time to acquire rotary skills, but it is
time well spent.

7. Select your thread and prepare the machine with a new, sharp needle.
Be certain that the machine is clean inside and out, and oiled.
Consult the owner's manual. A machine in good working order helps
to ensure good results.

8. Be certain you know where the ¼" (0.75cm) seam mark is on the
machine throat plate, or measure and mark your machine with a
piece of masking tape. Use of a ¼" (0.75cm) presser foot is helpful.
The cut edge of fabric along the seamline must ride on this mark or
along the edge of the presser foot. Use a setting on the sewing
machine that results in 10 to 12 stitches to the inch (4 to 5 stitches to
the cm). To sew a seam, stitch from cut edge to cut edge. If you are
working with similar shapes, you can chain-stitch a number of units
together at one time. Just continue feeding pieces under the presser
foot, with a stitch or two of thread between them (fig. 3.19). You do
not need to backstitch at the beginnings or ends of the seams
because another line of stitching will cross them.

For best results, start and stop the rotary
cutter on the mat, beyond the edges of
the fabric. Keep the rotary blade perpendicular to the edge of the ruler; don't let
it slant either toward or away from the
ruler (fig. 3.17). *Always close the cover
on the rotary cutter.* Get into the habit of
doing this each and every time you put
the cutter down.

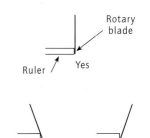

Figure 3.17

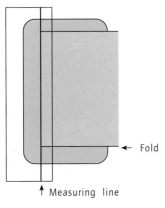

← Fold

↑ Measuring line

Figure 3.18

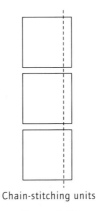

Chain-stitching units

Figure 3.19

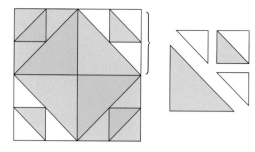

Figure 3.20

9. Sew the blocks together in units, following a piecing diagram when available. For example, the *Birds in the Air* block has four identical units—a large half-square triangle and four smaller half-square triangles (fig. 3.20). Stitch the smaller triangles into a larger triangle and sew this to the plain large triangle; repeat four times. The four units are sewn together, placing the large plain triangles in the center of the block. Most grid-based blocks are joined in horizontal, vertical, or diagonal rows. On occasion, stitched pieces will not fit together properly. In most instances, you can successfully ease the pieces together. You may hear this referred to as "the fudge factor." Use enough pins to secure, and stitch with the piece to be eased underneath, against the feed dogs. If the results just aren't satisfactory, you may need to recut a piece or two.

10. For a seamline that joins stitched units, pin the pieces together, carefully matching edges and seams. If possible, butt the matched seams: turn one seam allowance to the right and the other to the left (fig. 3.21). This allows the seams to "snug up" to each other. Help yourself here by *finger pressing* the seams (squeezing the seam flat with pressure between your thumb and fingers; do not drag your thumbnail along the seam). Pin before stitching. Keep the back side of your blocks neat. Clip threads to ¼" (0.75cm).

Allowance to left

Allowance to right

Seams meet

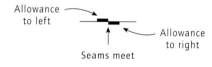

Figure 3.21

Now it's time to practice these techniques and learn some fun lessons about color while making the quilt projects in Chapter 4. You may choose to make only one block using each technique and pattern, assembling them into a sampler quilt, or you may make an entire small quilt from the blocks featuring a particular piecework shape. Should you be seized by uncontrollable ambition, why not try making the project again in a different fabric style or color scheme? Enjoy the possibilities!

Chapter 4

Piecework Projects

Before you begin working on any of the 10 piecework projects in this chapter, read the following general instructions. This could keep you from making unnecessary mistakes. Review the basic tools list to make sure you have everything you need so that you can work without interruptions.

PROJECT PREPARATION

Basic Guidelines

- Before beginning a project, read through all of the instructions for that pattern.
- All seams are sewn at ¼" (0.75cm) unless otherwise noted, with fabric right sides together.
- Prepare fabrics according to your preference before beginning.
- Measurement (unfinished) indicates that the block has been sewn together, but is not joined to anything else. It still retains the ¼" (0.75cm) seam allowance around its outside edge.
- Fabric requirements are estimated based on 42" (106cm) fabric width.
- Review the complete information in the general text on specific project topics, such as setting or quilting, before beginning that part of the project.
- Remember that accuracy counts and that attention to template and seam sizes will produce better results.
- Templates for all projects begin on page 128.
- All quilting suggestions are just that—you decide what best serves your quilt.

Hand Work Tips

- Cutting instructions are for *one* block, unless otherwise indicated.
- Stitch pieces point to point, passing the needle through any seam allowances.
- Because hand stitching doesn't sew down any crossing seams, pressing can be done after the block is assembled.

Machine Work Tips

- Cutting instructions are for the entire sample quilt size.
- Unless otherwise indicated, strips are cut crosswise (selvage to selvage).
- Remember to restraighten the fabric edge when rotary cutting strips and when recutting across sewn strip sets. Position a ruler line parallel to the folded edge or the seam lines.
- *Always* close the rotary cutter before it leaves your hand—even if only for a moment.
- Stitch cut edge to cut edge, unless otherwise indicated.
- Finger pressing (squeezing the seam flat with pressure between your thumb and fingers) as you work is useful. It allows you to position the seam without heavily creasing it.

Basic Tools List

Hand Work	Machine Work
Needles	Needles
sharps or milliner's/straw	80/12 universal or jeans/denim
betweens	80/12 long-eye
Thimble	Bobbins
Compatible thread	Specialty machine feet
Pins	Compatible thread
Scissors	Pins
utility	Scissors
fabric	utility
Fabric-marking pencils	fabric
Four-squares-to-the-inch (four-squares-to-the-cm) graph paper	Rotary cutter, mat, thick Plexiglas ruler
Template plastic	Four-squares-to-the-inch (four-squares-to-the-cm) graph paper
Quilter's quarter or ruler	Template plastic
Iron; board or mat	Seam ripper
Tape measure	Iron; board or mat
Chalk pencils	Tape measure
Quilting hoop or frame	Chalk pencils

Courthouse Steps

43″ × 56″ (107.5cm × 140cm); 30 blocks; 1 plain border

Jean A. Markowitz, Kent, Ohio ◆ machine pieced; machine quilted

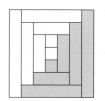

Courthouse Steps: half light and half dark— *Log Cabin* arrangement

Courthouse Steps: opposing light/dark— traditional arrangement

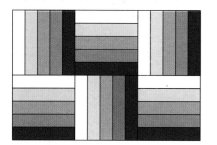

Rail Fence: light to dark value progression in each block

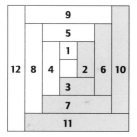

Log Cabin: half light and half dark; circular, incremental construction

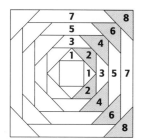

Pineapple: angled increments, alternating light and dark

Figure 4.1

Color Clues—Understanding Value

Value refers to the degree of lightness or darkness in any color. Contrasting values in a design establish distinctive shapes. These value contrasts have considerable visual impact, depending on the degree of contrast. As quiltmakers, we use value to delineate the geometric patterns in our quilts. Even the simple shapes of rectangles and squares can produce a quilt with great visual impact. Value placement creates the patterning in the straight-line blocks shown here (fig. 4.1).

Remember that value is always relative. It literally depends on how the fabrics relate to each other. Three arrangements are shown: one fabric is constant in each, but observe how its value changes.

Always test fabric selections to see how they work together. Just because all the fabrics are luscious individually doesn't mean that they will make a great team. A range of values as the fabrics are combined is essential.

The sample quilt colors are red, white (beige), and blue, always a popular color scheme. This quilt would be equally effective done all in one color family, or with a scrap look. *Value* is critical for both of these approaches.

Constant fabric changes value relative to other fabrics

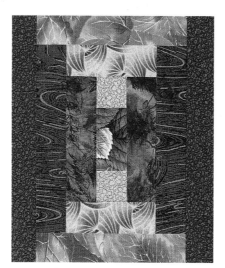 

Monochromatic traditional coloration

Scrap (multi-fabric) *Log Cabin* coloration

Fabric Requirements

Center	6″ (15cm) strip
4 lights	3/8 yd. (0.4m) each
4 darks	3/8 yd. (0.4m) each
Border	2 yds. (1.8m), cut lengthwise—for directional fabric
	1 yd. (0.7m), cut crosswise
Backing	2 yds. (1.8m)
Binding	1/2 yd. (0.5m)
Batting	45″ × 60″ (115cm × 150cm)

Cutting with Hand Work Templates

For each block as shown, mark and cut:

A	1 center, constant color
B to **G**	1 light and 1 dark

Rotary Cutting for Machine Piecing Based on 42″ (106cm) selvage to selvage

	Quantity	Size
From center fabric A, cut two 1 1/2″ (4cm) strips; recut into thirty 2 1/2″ × 1 1/2″ (6.5cm × 4cm) pieces.		
From each of four lights, cut	6 strips	1 1/2″ (4cm)
recut strips into a total of	30 **B**	1 1/2″ × 1 1/2″ (4cm × 4cm)
	30 **C**	1 1/2″ × 4 1/2″ (4cm × 11.5cm)
	30 **D**	1 1/2″ × 3 1/2″ (4cm × 9cm)
	30 **E**	1 1/2″ × 6 1/2″ (4cm × 16.5cm)
	30 **F**	1 1/2″ × 5 1/2″ (4cm × 14cm)
	30 **G**	1 1/2″ × 8 1/2″ (4cm × 21.5cm)
From each of four darks, cut	6 strips	1 1/2″ (4cm)
recut strips into a total of	30 **B**	1 1/2″ × 1 1/2″ (4cm × 4cm)
	30 **C**	1 1/2″ × 4 1/2″ (4cm × 11.5cm)
	30 **D**	1 1/2″ × 3 1/2″ (4cm × 9cm)
	30 **E**	1 1/2″ × 6 1/2″ (4cm × 16.5cm)
	30 **F**	1 1/2″ × 5 1/2″ (4cm × 14cm)
	30 **G**	1 1/2″ × 8 1/2″ (4cm × 21.5cm)
From border, cut	4 strips	4 1/2″ (11.5cm)

This quilt can be made with three fabrics—one center constant, one light, and one dark (repeat center for border); or with seven fabrics—one center, three lights, and three darks (repeat center for border). The sample is made from ten fabrics—one center, four lights, four darks, and one border (repeats center color, not fabric). It is much more visually interesting to keep changing the placement of the light and dark fabrics within their section of the block and to vary the combinations of the fabrics.

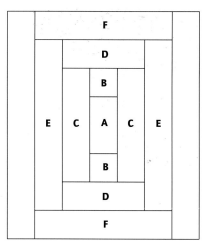

Figure 4.2

Hand Work

To hand piece the *Courthouse Steps* block, lay out pieces **A** to **G** to match the block diagram (fig. 4.2). Pin each step, right sides together, matching the marked seamlines. Stitch point to point, carefully following the seamlines. *Log Cabin* and traditional assemblies are shown (fig. 4.3).

When the block is assembled, press each seam toward the *last added piece*; for example, the seam of **A** + **B** is pressed toward **B**; the seam of **BAB** + **C** is pressed toward **C**.

This block measures 7½″ × 8½″ (18.5cm × 21cm), unfinished.

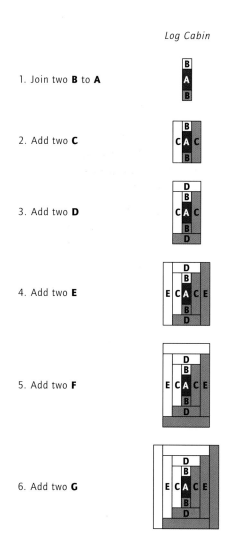

1. Join two **B** to **A**

2. Add two **C**

3. Add two **D**

4. Add two **E**

5. Add two **F**

6. Add two **G**

Figure 4.3

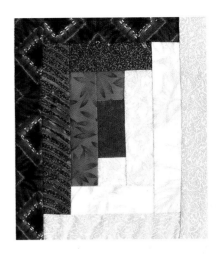

Machine Work

Machine piecing of this project can be approached in an assembly line fashion. Lay out stacks of all block pieces, **A** to **G**, to match the block diagram. Follow the same progression as illustrated for hand work. Remember that you are stitching from cut edge to cut edge.

1. Right sides together and using a ¼″ (0.75cm) seam, chain-piece half of the **B** pieces (30) to the **A** pieces. Clip the "stringing" threads to cut apart the sets. Chain-piece the other half of the **B** pieces to the opposite side of the **A** pieces. Cut apart the sets. Press seams toward the **B** pieces. Do this gently!

2. Chain-piece half of the **C** pieces (30) to the **BAB** sets. Cut apart the sets. Chain-piece the remaining **C** pieces to the opposite side of the **BAB** sets. Cut apart the sets. Press seams toward the **C** pieces. Gently . . .

3. Chain-piece half of the **D** pieces (30) to the **BABC** sets. Cut apart the sets. Chain-piece the remaining **D** pieces to the opposite side of the **BABC** sets. Cut apart the sets. Press seams toward the **D** pieces.

4. Chain-piece half of the **E** pieces (30) to the **BABCD** sets. Cut apart the sets. Chain-piece the remaining **E** pieces to the opposite side of the **BABCD** sets. Cut apart the sets. Press seams toward the **E** pieces. Are you keeping the seams straight and the edges square as you press?

5. Chain-piece half of the **F** pieces (30) to the **BABCDE** sets. Cut apart the sets. Chain-piece the remaining **F** pieces to the opposite sides of the **BABCDE** sets. Cut apart the sets. Press seams toward the **F** pieces.

6. Chain-piece half of the **G** pieces (30) to the **BABCDEF** sets. Cut apart the sets. Chain-piece the remaining **G** pieces to the opposite sides of the **BABCDEF** sets. Cut apart the sets. Press seams to the **G** pieces. The blocks should measure 7½″ × 8½″ (18.5cm × 21cm), unfinished. Aim to make the blocks consistent in size, as close as possible to the exact measurement.

Celebrate! Thirty blocks done!

Setting

1. Lay out blocks to match the quilt photo or try your own arrangement.
2. Pin and stitch five blocks, right sides together and matching seams, into each horizontal row. Repeat for a total of six rows.
3. Press the four seams, which join the blocks in each row, in opposite directions to aid in matching: all joint seams in Row **1** to the right, all in Row **2** to the left, etc. Join the horizontal rows, right sides together and matching seams.
4. Press the assembled blocks. Measure and cut the two side border pieces:

    _____ (length of side) × 4½″ (11cm) wide

    Join assembled blocks to side borders. Pin and stitch, right sides together, keeping the blocks on top whether stitching by hand or machine. Press the seams toward the border.
5. Measure and cut the top and bottom borders:

    _____ (length of side plus width of attached side borders) × 4½″ (11cm) wide

    Join assembled blocks to borders as in Step 4. Press the seams toward the border.

Backing, Quilting, and Binding

Make the quilt backing to measure 47″ × 60″ (117.5cm × 150cm). The backing will have to be pieced unless you have purchased 54″ or 60″ (138cm or 150cm) wide fabric.

Prepare the quilt for this process by basting the layers together. In-the-ditch is usually a good stitching plan for this type of quilt. Stitching across many seams by hand is not easy; it is less of a problem by machine. Stitch in-the-ditch between all blocks, horizontally and vertically. Also stitch in-the-ditch around the rectangle formed by pieces **A**, **B**, and **C**. Resist the temptation to stitch straight lines in the border and try some cables instead. The sample shows gentle curves stitched with an even-feed foot.

Make 6 yards (5.5m) of binding for your *Courthouse Steps* quilt.

All of the straight line block patterns make wonderful graphic quilts. You can try wider strips (needing fewer per block) or smaller blocks. Look at pictures of both antique and wildly contemporary quilts for inspiration. *Rail Fence*, *Courthouse Steps*, *Log Cabin*, and *Pineapple* are ageless!

Nine-Patch

43″ × 52″ (107cm × 128cm); 20 *Nine-Patch* blocks; 12 alternate blocks; 14 setting triangles; 4 corner triangles; 2 plain borders

Trish (Patti) Lenz, Cinebar, Washington ◆ machine pieced; machine quilted

Color Clues

Theme-related fabrics can be happily incorporated into your quilts. You will find holiday prints, landscapes, animals, and hobby interests. Look for fabrics with special motifs, such as hearts, shamrocks, pumpkins and fall foliage, flags, witches and ghosts, holiday decorations, sports equipment, children's toys, dogs, cats, birds or fish.

It's fun to have quilts for the beds or walls to decorate your home for a special season or to feature a family member's particular interest. *Nine-Patch* design quilts lend themselves to displaying these special fabrics.

Understanding print scale is a valuable quiltmaking skill. *Scale* refers to the size of the motifs on printed fabrics. To see the different shapes clearly in a block pattern, emphasize shapes in the pattern through placement of print scale, value, or color. In this project, four fabrics are used in the blocks. The red and green fabrics have an identical large poinsettia print, the beige fabric has a much smaller print, and the red-green mix fabric has a medium-size print. If the print scale of your fabrics is similar, then you must use color or value to differentiate the design shapes.

The sample blocks shown illustrate additional *Nine-Patch* block ideas. Note the print scale variations. Some methods for setting *Nine-Patch* blocks include on point (as in this project), straight with sashing, or straight with cornerstone sashing (fig. 4.4).

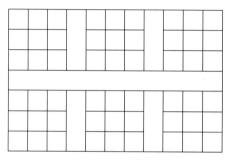

Straight setting with sashing

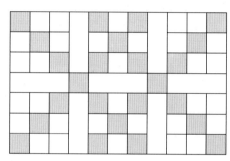

Straight setting with cornerstone sashing

Figure 4.4

A collection of theme-related fabrics

Fabric Requirements

Red	¼ yd. (0.3m)
Green	¼ yd. (0.3m)
Multicolor	¼ yd. (0.3m)
Beige	1½ yds. (1.5m)
Red border	⅜ yd. (0.3m)
Green border	1⅜ yds. (1.3m)
Backing	2⅔ yds. of 44" wide; 1½ yds. of 60" wide
	(2.4m of 111cm wide; 1.4m of 152cm wide)
Binding	½ yd. (0.5m)
Batting	45" × 60" (112cm × 152cm)

Cutting with Hand Work Templates

For each block, mark and cut:

A	2 red
	2 green
	1 multicolor
	4 beige

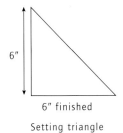
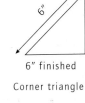

6" finished
Setting triangle

6" finished
Corner triangle

Figure 4.5a

Figure 4.5b

Make a setting triangle template based on the block measurements (fig. 4.5a). Mark and cut 14 beige. Make a corner triangle template based on the block measurements (fig. 4.5b). Mark and cut four beige.

Refer to page 7 for cutting corner and setting triangles.

You may elect to make corner and setting triangles using the rotary cutting instructions. Just remember to mark the seamlines at ¼" (0.75cm) from the cut edges.

Rotary Cutting for Machine Piecing Based on 42" (106cm) selvage to selvage

	Quantity	Size
From red print, cut	3 strips	2½" (6.5cm)
From green print, cut	3 strips	2½" (6.5cm)
From multicolor, cut	2 strips	2½" (6.5cm)
From beige, cut	7 strips	2½" (6.5cm)
	2 strips	6½" (16.5cm)
recut these two strips into	*12 squares*	*6½" (16.5cm)*
	1 square	7¼" (18.6cm)
recut square twice on diagonal to yield four corner triangles		
	7 squares	6⅞" (17.6cm)
recut squares once on diagonal to yield 14 side triangles		
From red border, cut	4 strips	2" (5cm)
From green border, cut	4 strips, lengthwise	3½" (9cm)

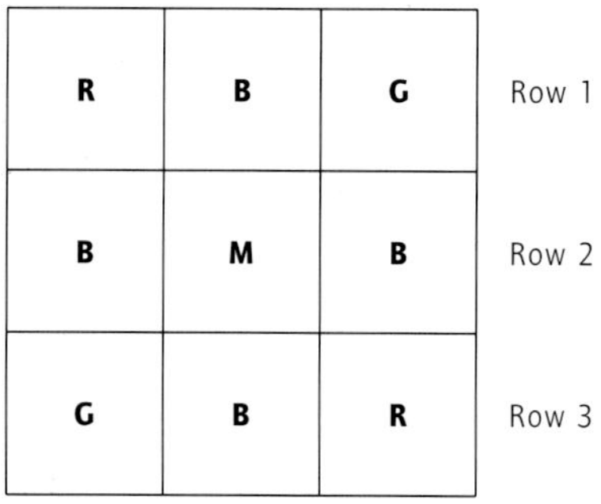

R	B	G	Row 1
B	M	B	Row 2
G	B	R	Row 3

Figure 4.6

Hand Work

To hand piece the *Nine-Patch* block, lay out pieces to match the drawing (fig. 4.6). Pin each step, right sides together, matching the marked seamlines. Stitch point to point, carefully following the seamlines.

1. Stitch these three rows as shown.
2. Matching seams, pin Rows **1** and **2**, right sides together. Stitch, remembering to pass the needle through the seam allowances at each joint.
3. Matching seams, pin Row **3** to the combined Rows **1** and **2**, right sides together. Stitch.
4. When the block is assembled, press the seams toward the dark fabric. This block measures 6½" (16.5cm) square, unfinished.

Machine Work

The *Nine-Patch* blocks for this project can be strip-pieced. This is a technique you will be able to use for many blocks or portions of blocks made from squares.

1. Right sides together, using a ¼″ (0.75cm) seam, sew one red and one beige strip together along one long cut edge. Repeat with two more red and beige strips for a total of three.
2. Sew a green strip, right sides together and using a ¼″ (0.75cm) seam, to the other long cut edge of the beige strip. Repeat with the remaining two strip sets (fig. 4.7).
3. Right sides together and using a ¼″ (0.75cm) seam, sew one beige and one multicolor strip together along one long cut edge. Repeat once more with a beige and a multicolor strip.
4. Sew a second beige strip to the other long cut edge of the multicolor strip. Repeat with the second strip set (fig. 4.8).
5. Press all five strip sets carefully from both sides—first the back, then the front. Press the seams toward the red, green, and multicolor fabrics. Seams should be straight, with no creases in the seamline on the right side.
6. Recut across all strip sets at 2½″ (6.5cm) intervals. Remember the following:

    ♦ First, straighten the end from which the cuts will be measured.
    ♦ Always keep a ruler line parallel to a seam.
    ♦ Check the cut edges often, keeping them at 90° to the seams.

    Cut 40 **RBG** sets. Cut 20 **BMB** sets (fig. 4.9).

7. Place one **BMB** set on top of an **RBG** set, right sides together, carefully matching seams. The seams will fit together nicely because of the direction in which they have been pressed. Chain-piece a total of 20 units. Clip the "stringing" threads to cut apart the units (fig. 4.10).
8. Open up the units and add another **RBG** set to the **BMB** side of the unit. Watch the placement: the **G** end of the set is now at the top (opposite **R**) (fig. 4.11). Chain-piece a total of 20 units. Cut apart the units. Press seams toward the **RBG** sets. The blocks should now measure 6½″ × 6½″ (16.5cm × 16.5cm) square.

Celebrate! Twenty blocks done!

Figure 4.7

Figure 4.8

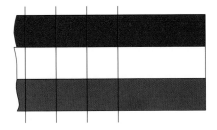

Figure 4.9

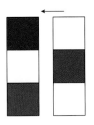

Figure 4.10

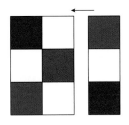

Figure 4.11

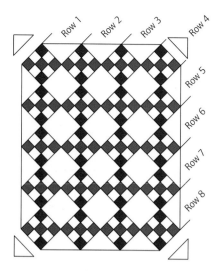

Figure 4.12

Setting

1. Lay out the blocks (both pieced and alternate), side triangles, and corner triangles as illustrated (fig. 4.12). Right sides together, matching corners and edges, stitch the blocks and triangles into diagonal rows, **1–8**. Press joining seams toward alternate blocks and setting triangles.

2. Matching seams and right sides together, join the diagonal rows, stitching **2** to **1**, **3** to **2**, and so on. Add the two remaining corner triangles. Press.

3. Measure and cut two red side border pieces:

_____ (length of side) × 2″ (5cm) wide

Right sides together, pin assembled blocks to border pieces. If the setting triangles were cut with the straight grain to the long side, pin with the triangles on top. If the setting triangles were cut with long sides on the bias, pin with the setting triangles underneath so that the bias edge is next to the feed dogs when machine piecing. Press the seam toward the border.

4. Measure and cut remaining two red border pieces:

_____ (length of side, including width of attached borders) × 2″ (5cm) wide

Join as above. Press seam toward the border.

5. Measure and cut two green side border pieces:

_____ (length of side, including width of attached borders) × 3½″ (9cm) wide

Pin and stitch to the sides of the quilt, right sides together. Press seams toward border.

6. Measure and cut remaining two green border pieces:

_____ (length of side, including width of attached borders) × 3½″ (9cm) wide

Pin and stitch to the top and bottom of the quilt, right sides together. Press seams toward border.

Backing, Quilting, and Binding

Make the quilt backing to measure 46″ × 54″ (120cm × 140cm). One piece of 54″ or 60″ (140cm or 150cm) fabric is sufficient, with the width of the fabric used as the lengthwise measurement of the backing. Sew two 44″ × 48″ (112cm × 122cm) pieces together to make a backing from 44″- (112cm-) wide fabric. Trim off the extra length.

Prepare the quilt for this process by basting the layers together. The open (alternate) blocks provide lots of space to quilt a specific design, such as a flower. Stitch in-the-ditch to secure all diagonal seamlines. Stitch the blocks in-the-ditch, at ¼″ (0.75cm) intervals, or with horizontal and vertical lines through the centers of the colored squares. Use cables or seasonal designs on the outside borders.

Make 5½ yards (5m) of binding for your *Nine-Patch* quilt.

The *Nine-Patch* is a wonderful pattern for featuring all sorts of specialty fabrics. Have fun collecting and displaying these in your quilts. You might also like to investigate the many ways that Amish quilters use the *Nine-Patch*. You are sure to find lots of ideas!

Birds in the Air

46″ × 54″ (115cm × 135cm); 20 blocks; 2 plain borders

Alison L. Curran, Tinton Falls, New Jersey ◆ machine pieced; machine quilted

Color Clues—Understanding Intense Hues and Tones

To alter the intensity of a pure color, the same value of gray is added to that color, in increasing amounts, until the hue itself has become gray. All of those steps between the pure color and gray are called *tones*.

    In addition to value and pattern scale, another way to achieve contrast in defining geometric quilt patterns is to use both strong and weak colors. This quilt is created with brights and tones of the same colors—fuchsia, green, purple, yellow, and blue. The combination is soft, yet dynamic.

    It is certainly possible to create a pleasing quilt with all brights or all tones; in doing so, the contrast must come from other factors. All brights will probably require separation by a neutral to create pattern definition. All tones can easily blend into "mush." Careful attention to color choice or value will be needed to provide enough contrast.

    The sample blocks illustrate brights—with and without a neutral—and tones—with and without value definition.

No contrast   Contrast   No contrast   Contrast

Tones (weak chroma)   Brights (strong chroma)

Combination of tones

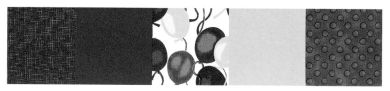

High chroma color fabrics

Fabric Requirements

Blocks	ten ¼ yd. (0.3m)—5 brights, 5 tones
Inner border	¼ yd. (0.3m)
Outer border	1⅜ yds. (1.3m)
Backing	1½ yds. of 60"-wide fabric (1.5m of 152cm-wide fabric), or
	2⅛ yds. of 44"-wide fabric (2.1m of 112cm-wide fabric)
Binding	¾ yd. (0.7m)
Batting	72" × 90" (183cm × 229cm)

Cutting with Hand Work Templates

For each block, mark and cut:

4 **E**	2 light (bright) and 2 dull (tone)
4 each **A**, **B**, **C**, **D**	8 light (bright) and 8 dull (tone)

There are only two templates for this block. **A**, **B**, **C**, and **D** are all cut from the same smaller triangle template.

Select and cut your fabrics either by carefully planning the placement of each color or by cutting random amounts of each fabric and template shape. Then shuffle the pieces and see if serendipity created an interesting mix! Make any changes before stitching.

Rotary Cutting for Machine Piecing Based on 42" (106cm) selvage to selvage

	Quantity	*Size*
For **E**, cut a total of	5 strips	4⅞" (12.6cm)
recut strips into a total of	*40 squares*	*4⅞" (12.6cm)*
recut each square once on diagonal to yield two half-square right triangles, for a total of 80		
For **A–D**, cut a total of	12 strips	2⅞" (7.6cm)
recut strips into a total of	*160 squares*	*2⅞" (7.6cm)*
recut each square once on diagonal to yield two half-square right triangles, for a total of 320		
For inner border, cut	4 strips, crosswise	1½" (4cm)
For outer border, cut	4 strips, lengthwise	6½" (16.5cm)

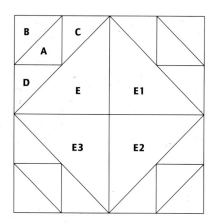

Figure 4.13

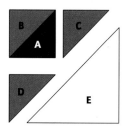

Figure 4.14

Hand Work

To hand piece the *Birds in the Air* block, lay out pieces **A** to **E3** to match the drawing (fig. 4.13). Pin each step, right sides together, matching the marked seamlines. Stitch point to point, carefully following the seamlines. One section of this block is constructed and repeated to form the complete block.

1. Following the construction diagram, join pieces **A** and **B**. Repeat three times, once for each remaining quarter.
2. Add piece **C** to unit **AB**. Repeat three times.
3. Add piece **D** to **ABC**. Repeat three times.
4. Add piece **E** to **ABCD** (fig. 4.14). Pin the **DC** lines on top of the **E** line, and stitch with **DC** facing you. Remember to pass the needle through the seam allowance. Repeat three times.
5. Stitch **E** to **E1**. Repeat for **E2** to **E3**.
6. Stitch **E–E1** to **E2–E3**, matching the seam. When the block is assembled, press seams toward **B**, **C**, **D**, and **E**. Press the **E** seams toward the dark, if possible. This block measures 8½″ (21.5cm) square, unfinished.

When you work with triangles, there are always extra long seam allowances at the tips of the angles. These are often called "dog ears." After a seam is completed, it is wise to trim these dog ears even with the ¼″ (0.75cm) seam allowance, to remove any extra bulk in the seams. This can also be done before seams are sewn by using a point trimmer tool and a rotary cutter. See Appendix 2 on page 126.

Machine Work

This project can also be approached in an assembly line manner. Stitch all pieces, right sides together, using a ¼" (0.75cm) seam.

1. Stack all **B** pieces, right sides up, to the left of the machine. Place the long sides of the triangle to the right, parallel to the presser foot. Stack all **A** pieces, wrong sides up (fig. 4.15). Placing one **A** piece on top of one **B**, chain 4 sets for each block, stitching the long sides together.
2. Cut apart the sets by clipping the "stringing" stitches, and open up the sets to form a square. Finger press the seam toward **B** by squeezing the seam flat with pressure between your thumb and fingers; do not drag your thumbnail along the seam. This is a bias edge and you don't want to stretch it. Carefully trim the dog ears (fig. 4.16).
3. Stack **AB** squares, right sides up, to the left of the machine as shown (fig. 4.17). Stack **C** triangles, wrong sides up, as shown (fig. 4.17). Matching the square corners, chain **C** to all **AB** sets. Remember that the bottom tip of triangle **C** will extend below square **AB** at the seamline.
4. Cut apart **ABC** units, and open out triangle **C**. Finger press the seam toward **C**.
5. Stack **D** triangles, right sides up, as shown (fig. 4.18). Stack units **ABC**, wrong sides up, as shown (fig. 4.18). Place one **ABC** on one **D**, and chain the units. Remember, the point of triangle **D** will extend below the corner of square **AB** at the seamline. Stitch a total of 4 units for each block.
6. Cut apart the units, and open out triangle **D**. Gently press the entire unit with the seam toward **D**. Don't stretch the unit. Trim the dog ears.
7. Join a triangle **E** to each of four **ABCD** units, carefully matching the long sides. Pin and stitch.
8. Pin **E** and **E1** together, matching corners. It may help the pieces to fit more snugly if seam **E** is pressed toward unit **ABCD** and seam **E1** is pressed toward triangle **E1**. Stitch. Repeat with **E2** and **E3**, seam **E2** pressed toward **ABCD** and seam **E3** pressed toward **E3**.
9. Pin unit **E–E1** to unit **E2–E3**, matching seams. Stitch. The block measures 8½" (21.5cm) square, unfinished. Repeat for a total of 20 blocks. Celebrate!

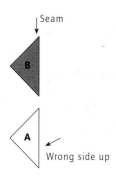

Figure 4.15

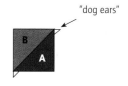

Figure 4.16

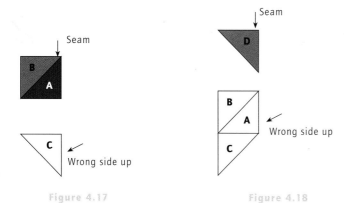

Figure 4.17

Figure 4.18

Setting

Lay out the blocks in a pleasing arrangement, four blocks wide by five blocks long.

1. Stitch four blocks together in a horizontal row, matching seams. Some seams will be pressed in the same direction when they meet, unavoidable with machine piecing. Pin these joints securely, assisting the extra bulk through and under the presser foot when necessary. Repeat for a total of five rows.

2. Press the block-joining seams in each row in alternating directions—Rows **1**, **3**, and **5** to the right, and Rows **2** and **4** to the left. This will aid in matching seam intersections. Join the horizontal rows.

3. Press the assembled blocks. Measure and cut two side inner border pieces:

   _____ (length of side) $\times$ 1½" (4cm) wide

   Join assembled blocks to side inner borders. Pin and stitch, keeping the blocks on top whether stitching by hand or machine. Press seams toward borders.

4. Measure and cut two remaining inner border pieces:

   _____ (length of side, including width of attached borders) $\times$ 1½" (4cm) wide

   Join blocks to borders as in Step 3. Press seams toward borders.

5. Measure and cut two outer side borders:

   _____ (length of side, including width of attached borders) $\times$ 6½" (16.5cm) wide

   Join borders to sides. Pin and stitch. Press seams toward borders.

6. Measure and cut two remaining outer borders:

   _____ (length of side, including width of attached borders) $\times$ 6½" (16.5cm) wide

   Join borders to top and bottom. Pin and stitch. Press seams toward borders.

Backing, Quilting, and Binding

Make the quilt backing to measure 50" $\times$ 58" (127cm $\times$ 147cm). The backing will have to be pieced, unless you have purchased 60"- (152cm-) wide fabric, in which case the width can be used as the length of the backing.

Prepare the quilt by basting the layers together. Stabilize the quilt by stitching in-the-ditch between all blocks. Also stitch in-the-ditch along all **E** seamlines. To complete the blocks, highlight the four "bird" shapes by stitching at the quarter inch, or center a 7" (18cm) diameter floral design in the block and overlay the straight piecework with these curving lines. Stitch in-the-ditch around the inner border.

Make 6 yards (5.5m) of binding for your *Birds in the Air* quilt.

Block patterns featuring half-square triangles are my favorite. I especially love *Ocean Waves*. If you are intrigued by the special sparkle of these blocks, you might want to try one or more of the following: *Corn and Beans, Lady of the Lake, Delectable Mountains,* or *Lost Ships*. Remember to experiment with using brights and tones in your color selections.

Ohio Star

60″ × 60″ (153cm × 153cm); 25 blocks; sashing; 1 plain border

Jean A. Markowitz, Kent, Ohio ◆ machine pieced; machine quilted

Color Clues—Achromatic, Monochromatic, Polychromatic Harmonies

This quilt design was developed to illustrate a combination of the three harmonies based on color and because it was fun! Three different quilts could also be created—one made from all black, white, and gray (*achromatic*); one made from many values of a single color (*monochromatic*); and one made from all multicolor fabrics (*polychromatic*). Another approach, with a different color in every star, would also be called polychromatic.

This quilt is organized with warm colors on one side and cool colors on the other. Notice how the neutral block background and sashing (black and gray) allow each individual star fabric to shine without competition. Neutrals are effectively used to set off busy fabrics and multicolor schemes. A block placement diagram of the quilt is provided (fig. 4.19). It was a fun challenge to select fabrics to make the transition rows.

Once again, *value* plays an important role in creating a design. For the achromatic and monochromatic arrangements to be visually effective, you must use a range of values. The achromatic fabrics move from white, with a small amount of black pattern, to black, with a small amount of white pattern. The most simple monochromatic arrangement requires at least three values of one color—light, medium, and dark. The scales illustrate value progressions for both of these harmonies.

You can see the many possibilities that exist for selecting your quilt fabrics based on one or more of these harmonies.

Achromatic   Monochromatic

Polychromatic

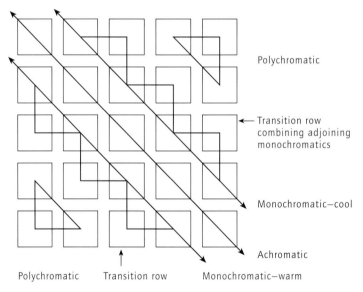

Polychromatic

Transition row combining adjoining monochromatics

Monochromatic—cool

Achromatic

Polychromatic   Transition row   Monochromatic—warm

Figure 4.19

Fabric Requirements

Stars	1³⁄₈ yds. (1.3m)
	to make individual stars, one 9" (24cm) square each
Background	2 yds. (2m)
Sashing and borders	1⅞ yds. (1.7m)
Backing	3 yds. (3m)
Binding	¾ yd. (0.7m)
Batting	72" × 90" (183cm × 129cm)

Cutting with Hand Work Templates

For each block, mark and cut:

	Template	Quantity
Background	**A**	4
	B	8
Star	**AS**	1
	BS	8

An optional color arrangement in these blocks changes the triangles that surround the center square (**AS**) from background to a third color. This gives the impression of a square on point in the center of the star. To create this, mark and cut:

Background	**A**	4
	B	4
Option	**BO**	4

The star pieces remain the same.

Rotary Cutting for Machine Piecing Based on 42" (106cm) selvage to selvage

	Quantity	Size
From background, cut	9 strips	3½" (9.5cm)
recut strips into	*100 squares* **A**	*3½" (9.5cm)*
From background, cut	6 strips	4¼" (11.6cm)
recut strips into	*50 squares*	*4¼" (11.6cm)*
recut each square twice on the diagonal to yield four quarter-square triangles,		
for a total of 200 **B**		
From star fabrics, cut	3 strips	3½" (9.5cm)
recut strips into	*25 squares* **AS**	*3½" (9.5cm)*
From star fabrics, cut	6 strips	4¼" (11.6cm)
recut strips into	*50 squares*	*4¼" (11.6cm)*
recut each square twice on the diagonal to yield four quarter-square triangles,		
for a total of 200 **BS**		
From sashing/border fabric, cut	8 strips, lengthwise	2" (5.5cm)
	4 strips, lengthwise	5" (13.5cm)

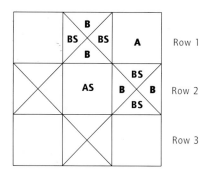

Figure 4.20

Figure 4.21

Hand Work

To hand piece the *Ohio Star* block, lay out pieces **A** and **B** to match the drawing (fig. 4.20). Pin each step, right sides together, matching the marked seamlines. Stitch point to point, carefully following the seamlines.

1. Join **B1** to **BS1**. Join **BS2** to **B2**. Repeat three times for the remaining star points.
2. Join the **B1**–**BS1** unit to **B2**–**BS2** to form a square (fig. 4.21). Match seams; pass the needle through the seam allowance. Repeat three times.
3. Stitch Row **1**. Join one **A** to the left of the **B**–**BS** unit and one **A** to the right. Watch the placement. **A** is stitched to **BS**. Repeat for Row **3**.
4. Stitch Row **2**. Join one **B**–**BS** unit to the left of the **AS** square and one to the right. Watch the placement. **AS** is stitched to **B**.
5. Join Row **1** to Row **2**, matching seams. Join Row **3** to Row **2**.
6. Press seams to the dark when possible. Trim dog ears.

Note: It is not always possible to press seams toward the darker fabric. Sometimes the seams will find a more "comfortable" direction for themselves, and when we try to press them in another direction, bunching and shifting occurs. At other times, it's an even better idea to press a seam open to help pieces lay flatter. Use good judgment and common sense when pressing. Fabrics are like children—gentle coercion often produces better results than force!

This block measures 9½″ (25.5cm) square, unfinished.

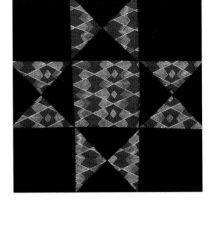

Machine Work

You may choose to chain-piece one block at a time or do assembly line work for all blocks at once. This will depend greatly on your overall scheme. If all pieces are identical, you can stitch all the units at one time.

1. Stack all **B** pieces, right sides up, to the left of the machine as shown (fig. 4.22). Stack all **BS** pieces, wrong sides up. Place one **BS** on top of one **B** to make one set. Chain 8 sets for each block (fig. 4.22).

2. Cut apart the sets by clipping the "stringing" threads. Join two **B**–**BS** sets, right sides together and matching seams to make one unit (fig. 4.23). Turn all seams toward either **B** or **BS**—just be consistent. Repeat for a total of four units for each block. Make all **B**–**BS** units before moving to Step 3. Press and trim dog ears.

3. Chain together the following sequence: **A** and **BS**–**B**, **B**–**BS** and **AS**, **A** and **BS**–**B**, as shown (fig. 4.24).

4. Open each unit. Chain on, in this order: **A**, **BS**–**B**, and **A**, as shown (fig. 4.25).

5. Rotate the block one-quarter turn to the right, as shown (fig. 4.26). Right sides together, turn Row **1** over Row **2**, matching seam intersections and turning seams toward **A** and **AS** pieces. Pin as necessary. Stitch edge to edge.

6. Rotate the block 180°, as shown (fig. 4.27). Turn Row **3** over Row **2**, matching seam intersections and turning seams toward **A** and **AS** pieces. Pin as necessary. Stitch edge to edge.

This block measures 9½" (26.5cm) square, unfinished. Congratulations! Only 24 more blocks to go! This is a great method for assembling blocks that can be sewn together in straight rows. Make all individual units first; then chain-piece the rows.

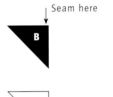

Figure 4.22

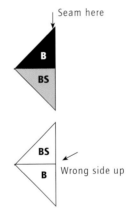

Figure 4.23

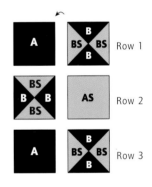

Figure 4.24

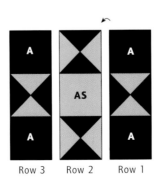

Figure 4.25

Figure 4.26

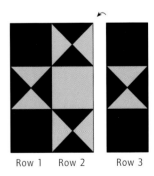

Figure 4.27

Setting

1. Lay out the blocks to match the quilt photo or make your own arrangement.
2. Measure and cut 20 vertical sashing pieces:

   _____ (length of unfinished block) × 2″ (5.5cm) wide

3. Join blocks to sashing pieces, right sides together, keeping the block on top. For hand work, continuing to stitch point to point will keep the star points from becoming truncated. For machine work, this seam should just skim the X formed by the triangle-point seams. You may need to stitch a thread's width past this X onto the seam allowance side to prevent the point of the triangle from disappearing. Press seams toward the sashing. Repeat for a total of five rows.

4. Measure and cut four horizontal sashing pieces:

   _____ (length of row, including width of attached sashing) × 2″ (5.5cm) wide

5. Join rows to sashing pieces. Keep rows on top. Press seams toward sashing. Remember to measure carefully as you add each row to keep the blocks lined up vertically.

6. Measure and cut two side borders:

   _____ (length of side) × 5″ (13.5cm) wide

   Join sashed blocks to side borders. Pin and stitch, keeping blocks on top. Press seams toward borders.

7. Measure and cut two remaining borders:

   _____ (length of side, including width of attached borders) × 5″ (13.5cm) wide

   Join sashed blocks to top and bottom borders as above. Press seams toward borders.

Backing, Quilting, and Binding

Make the quilt backing to measure 64″ (164cm) square. The backing will have to be pieced on one edge.

Prepare the quilt by basting the layers together. Because there are many colors and fabrics in this design, the quilting is straight and simple. The entire quilt is crisscrossed by straight lines of stitching that follow the X made in the star point units. Dark transparent thread, which blends with the fabric, was used to stitch in-the-ditch of the star point units and across the sashing and border. For different color treatments, you may choose to stitch at the ¼″ (0.75cm) within the stars, and showcase linear stitching patterns such as cables or vines in the sashing and border. Or you may choose to cover the entire surface with randomly quilted stars.

Make 7 yards (6.4m) of binding for your *Ohio Star* quilt.

If you enjoyed making the *Ohio Star*, you might like to try some of its relatives: *Swamp Patch* (don't ask! I have no idea why it has this name), *Silent Star*, and *Combination Star*. Each would make a beautiful quilt by itself or a wonderful four-block sampler could be made using all of them.

Grandma's Star

52″ × 52″ (128cm × 128cm); 5 blocks; 2 plain borders

Lynn G. Kough, Chandler, Arizona ◆ machine pieced; machine quilted

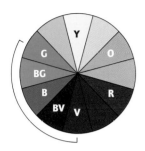

Figure 4.28

Color Clues

Noted color theorist Faber Birren commented that "analogous colors have an emotional quality . . . ," while another colorist observed that "the close relationship of the colors readily suggests a dominant mood or idea." Many quilts exhibit analogous harmonies, whether by accident or by design. The color combinations are "comfortable" to work with and to view.

Analogous means closely related. Using colors that touch or are closely positioned on the color wheel results in an analogous color harmony for your quilt. Base your color grouping on a primary (red, yellow, or blue) or a secondary (orange, violet, or green) color. The most basic analogous harmony uses one color plus the colors immediately to its left and right on the wheel (violet, blue-violet, red-violet).

The fabrics for the sample quilt were selected from a base of blue (fig. 4.28). Because blue and violet are colors I associate with memories of my grandmother, and we share green as the color of our birthstone, this kind of color scheme worked well for the project. For those who like cool colors, a grouping of blue-violet, blue-green, and blue is often a favorite. I love hot colors in a combination of red, red-orange, and red-violet. Remember that these groupings may include tints, shades, or tones as well as the pure colors. Two possible combinations are shown—one cool, one hot. What analogous combinations do you find pleasing?

Analogous cool colors

Analogous hot colors

Fabric Requirements

Stars	6″ (15cm) strip each of five fabrics
Light background	1¼ yds. (1.3m)
Dark background	¼ yd. (0.3m)
Inner border	½ yd. (0.5m)
Outer border	2 yds. (2m) directional fabric or 1½ yds. (2m) nondirectional, cut lengthwise
Backing	1⅝ yds. of 60″-wide fabric (1.6m of 152cm-wide fabric)
	2½ yds. of 44″-wide fabric (2.5m of 112cm-wide fabric)
Binding	½ yd. (0.5m)
Batting	72″ × 90″ (183cm × 229cm)

The print direction of the fabric used for the border in this quilt dictates that two strips are cut crosswise and two lengthwise. Examine your own fabrics before you cut to determine if the print has a direction.

Cutting with Hand Work Templates

For each block, mark and cut:

	Template	Quantity
Background (light)	**A**	8
	B	4
Center block only—no **A**	**D**	4
Background (dark)	**A**	8
Star	**C**	4
	CR	4
	D	1

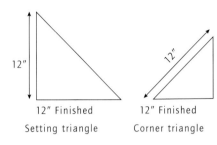

12″   12″

12″ Finished   12″ Finished
Setting triangle   Corner triangle

Figure 4.29

Make a setting triangle template based on the block measurements (fig. 4.29). Mark and cut four background. Make a corner triangle template based on the block measurements. Mark and cut four background. You may elect to make corner and setting triangles using the rotary cutting instructions. Just remember to mark the seamlines at ¼″ (0.75cm) from the cut edges.

Note: Templates are marked **C** and **CR**. This means to mark and cut the fabric first with the template facing one way; then reverse the template (turn it over—which makes a mirror image) and mark and cut the fabric this way. Often you will see instructions with a template that say "Cut one, cut one reverse." Now you know what to do!

Rotary Cutting for Machine Piecing Based on 42″ (106cm) selvage to selvage

	Quantity	Size
From light background, cut:	2 strips **A**	2½″ (6.5cm)
	4 squares (center block corners)	4½″ (11.5cm)
	2 strips	4½″ (11.5cm)
*recut into 20 template **B** triangles*		
	1 strip	13¼″ (35cm)
recut this strip into	3 squares; 2 squares are	12⅞″ (32.6cm)
	*then recut once on the diagonal to yield four side triangles **E***	
	1 square remains	13¼″ (35cm)
*recut this square twice on the diagonal to yield four corner triangles **F***		
From dark background, cut	2 strips **A**	2½″ (6.5cm)
From each of five star fabrics, cut	1 strip	4½″ (11.5cm)
recut each strip into	1 square	4½″ (11.5cm)
	4	Template **C**
	4	Template **CR**
From inner border, cut	4 strips	3¼″ (8.5cm)
From outer border, cut	2 strips	6½″ (16.5cm)
	2 strips	6½″ × 54″ (16.5cm × 137cm)

The templates for this project are provided in inches only. If you are working in centimeters, your may need to adjust the seam allowances, using as narrow as a 0.5cm seam allowance for the template pieces, as necessary. If in doubt, when you match up rotary-cut pieces with template-cut pieces prior to sewing, always use the rotary cut piece as a guide to final measurement. For absolute accuracy, use templates rather than rotary cutting, just as you would if you were hand-making the block.

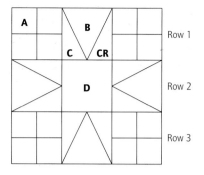

Row 1

Row 2

Row 3

Figure 4.30

Hand Work

To hand piece the *Grandma's Star* block (also known as a variation of *54–40 or Fight*), lay out pieces **A**, **B**, **C**, **CR**, and **D** to match the drawing (fig. 4.30). Note that the center block of the quilt does not use **A** pieces in the four corners. Instead, four **D** pieces are cut from the background for the corners. Pin each step, right sides together, matching the marked seamlines. Stitch point to point, carefully following the marked seamlines. A progression of squares through a block and across a quilt is often called a chain. You will see that design element in this project and in Project 6, *Blackford's Beauty*.

1. Join one dark **A** to one light **A**. Repeat. Join one **AA** unit to the other **AA** unit, matching the seam and again stitching a dark **A** to a light **A**. Repeat for the other three corners. Press the seams to the darks where possible.

2. Join one **C** to **B** as shown. Join one **CR** to the other side of **B**. Repeat three times for the other star points. Press the seams toward **C**. Repeat for Row **3**.

It is a good idea to mark the base of triangle **B**, both on the template and all fabric pieces. The three sides are so similar that it is easy to begin attaching **C** to the incorrect side.

3. Stitch Row **1**. Join one **AA** unit to the left of a **BC** unit and one **AA** to the right. Watch the placement. The dark **A** corner must be stitched to the base of **C** (or toward the center of the block) on both sides. Check that the skinny star points (**C**) are pointing to the *outside* of the block on all four sides. Repeat for Row **3**.

4. Stitch Row **2**. Join one **BC** unit to the left of the **D** square and one to the right. Watch the placement. **D** is stitched to the base of **C** on both sides.

5. Join Row **1** to Row **2**, matching seams. Join Row **3** to Row **2**.

6. Press seams to the dark when possible. Trim dog ears.

This block measures 12½″ (31.5cm) square, unfinished.

Machine Work

The small **A** units can be strip-pieced, just as the blocks were in Project 2, *Nine-Patch* (fig. 4.31). It is possible to chain-piece the star point units (**BC**), but care must be taken to correctly place the **C** unit.

1. Right sides together and using a ¼" (0.75cm) seam, sew one light (background) and one dark strip together along one long cut edge. Repeat. Press both strip sets carefully from both sides—first the back, then the front. Press the seams toward the dark fabric. Seams should be straight, with no creases in the seam-line on the right side. Recut across all strip sets at 2½" (6.5cm) intervals (fig. 4.32). Cut 32 **AA** sets.

2. Join two **AA** sets to make one corner unit. Place one **AA** right sides together on another **AA**, making sure that a light is always paired with a dark. Chain 16 units. Cut the units apart and press.

3. Join all **C** pieces to all **B** pieces. Remember, the base of one is always next to the point of the other (fig. 4.33). The top (or point) of the **B** template is cut off to help show this placement.

4. Cut apart the **CB** sets, open out the **C** triangles and finger press the seams toward **C**. Join all **CR** pieces to all **CB** sets. Again take care aligning the pieces. Cut apart the **CBCR** units and carefully press the seams toward **C** and **CR**.

5. Chain together the following sequence: **AA** and **CBCR**, **CBCR** and **D**, **AA** and **CBCR**, as shown (fig. 4.34). Watch the placement of dark small squares and star points.

6. Open each unit. Chain on, in this order—**AA**, **CBCR**, and **AA**—as shown (see fig. 4.34).

7. Rotate the block one-quarter turn to the right. Right sides together, turn Row **1** over Row **2**, matching seams and turning the Step 5 and 6 seams toward **AA** and **D** pieces. Pin as necessary. Stitch edge to edge.

8. Rotate the block 180°. Turn Row **3** over Row **2**, matching seams and turning seams as above. Pin as necessary. Stitch edge to edge. Congratulations! Only four more blocks to go! Remember, the center block has no **AA** units. This block measures 12½" (33.5cm) square, unfinished.

Note: It is very important to match these pieces correctly so that a proper seam allowance will be formed where pieces **C** and **CR** cross each other. The angle at the point of **C** on the template will match the base of **B** for a correct fit.

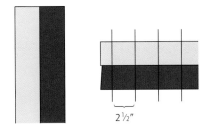

Figure 4.31   Figure 4.32

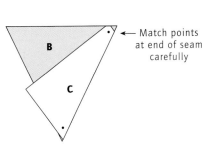

B

C

← Match points at end of seam carefully

Figure 4.33

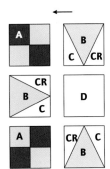

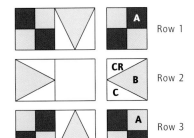

Figure 4.34

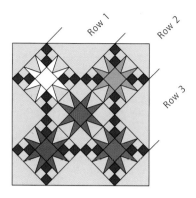

Figure 4.35

Split-square stars are fascinating! I like this block placed on point, where it reminds me of a Maltese cross. Another wonderful block made with these skinny points is *Storm at Sea*. Use split-square triangles to create illusions of curved lines. When you feel really adventurous, try Jinny Beyer's block, *California Sunset*.

Setting

1. Lay out blocks, setting triangles, and corner triangles to match the quilt photo. Right sides together, matching corners, edges, and seams, stitch the blocks and triangles into diagonal Rows **1**, **2**, and **3** (fig. 4.35). Press joining seams toward setting triangles and the center block.

2. Matching seams and right sides together, join the diagonal rows: **1 → 2 → 3**. Add the remaining corner triangles. Press.

3. Measure and cut two side inner border pieces:

   _____ (length of side) × 3¼″ (8.5cm) wide

   Pin and stitch, right sides together. Press the seams toward the plain border. Measure and cut the two remaining inner border pieces.

   _____ (length of side, including attached border pieces) × 3¼″ (8.5cm) wide

   Pin and stitch, right sides together. Press the seams toward the plain border.

4. Measure and cut the two side outer border pieces. If you have directional fabric, cut the two 6½″ (16.5cm) strips across the fabric (for the top and bottom borders) before cutting the lengthwise side borders.

   _____ (length of side, including width of attached borders) × 6½″ (16.5cm) wide

   Pin and stitch, right sides together. Press the seams toward the outer border.

5. Measure and cut the two remaining outer border pieces.

   _____ (length of side, including width of attached border pieces) × 6½″ (16.5cm) wide

   Pin and stitch, right sides together. Press the seams toward the outer border.

Backing, Quilting, and Binding

Make the quilt backing to measure 56″ × 56″ (142cm × 142cm). The backing will have to be pieced unless you have purchased 60″-wide (152cm-wide) fabric.

Prepare the quilt by basting the layers together. Stabilize the quilt by stitching in-the-ditch between all blocks. Continue stitching in this fashion along the lines formed by the center square of the stars. These lines can continue right into Border 1 and Border 2 if you desire. Or stitch inside the stars at the quarter inch, as well as the dark background squares. Stitch triangular motifs in the setting and corner triangles. Stitch diamond cables in the outside border. Basically, you must choose whether to accentuate the angularity of the pieces or stitch curves to soften the sharp edges. Either choice will be just fine!

Make 6 yards (5.5m) of binding for your *Grandma's Star* quilt.

Blackford's Beauty

39″ × 39″ (99cm × 99cm); 4 blocks; sashing with pieced cornerstones; 1 plain border

Trish (Patti) Lenz, Cinebar, Washington ◆ machine pieced; machine quilted

Color Clues—Using Complementary Colors

Complementary colors are found opposite each other on the color circle. Every color has its complement, and these color schemes are often a powerful contrast of opposing colors. The most familiar pairings are red and green, blue and orange, yellow and violet. At full saturation, these combinations are quite intense. Often, adding or substituting tints or shades of the complement results in a more pleasing visual combination. Think of cobalt blue sky with hints of peach, yellow pansies with deep violet faces, and bright red ribbons against dark green pine trees.

Another way to handle complementaries is to add a neighboring color from the circle. The project quilt features a sophisticated red-green combination with a soft peach (red-orange) block background and sashing. The black print ties it all together. Other less common, but equally fine, combinations are blue-green and red-orange, yellow-green and red-violet, yellow-orange and blue-violet.

Consider using some of the complementary pairings shown in the sample blocks. Remember that a complement can intensify your entire quilt color scheme or be used as a powerful accent.

Fabric Requirements

Background and sashing	1 yd. (1m)
Chain	³⁄₈ yd. (0.3m)
Center star and border	¾ yd. (0.7m)
Extended star points	³⁄₈ yd. (0.3m)
Backing	1¼ yds. (1.3m)
Binding	½ yd. (0.5m)
Batting	45″ × 60″ (114cm × 152cm)

Cutting with Hand Work Templates

For each block as shown, mark and cut:

	Template	Quantity
Background (light)	**A**	8
Chain (dark)	**A**	12
Background	**B**	8
Star	**C**	1
Star	**D**	8
Extended star	**E, ER**	4 each
Background	**F**	4

Rotary Cutting for Machine Piecing Based on 42″ (106cm) selvage to selvage

	Quantity	Size
From background fabric, cut	5 strips	2″ (5.5cm)
	1 strip	4¼″ (11.6cm)
recut strip into	*4 squares*	*4¼″ (11.6cm)*
recut squares twice on diagonal for a total of 16 **F** *triangles*		
	4 strips for sashing	3½″ (9.5cm)
From chain fabric, cut	4 strips	2″ (5.5cm)
	1 square	3½″ (9.5cm)
From star fabric, cut	1 strip	3½″ (9.5cm)
recut strip into	*4 squares*	*3½″ (9.5cm)*
	1 strip	2³⁄₈″ (6.6cm)
recut strip into	*16 squares*	*2³⁄₈″ (6.6cm)*
recut squares once on diagonal for a total of 32 **D** *triangles*		
	4 strips for border	3½″ (9.5cm)
From extended star fabric, cut	4 strips	2″ (5.5cm)

The templates for this project are provided in inches only. If you are working in centimeters, your may need to adjust the seam allowances, using as narrow as a 0.5cm seam allowance for the template pieces, as necessary. If in doubt, when you match up rotary-cut pieces with template-cut pieces prior to sewing, always use the rotary cut piece as a guide to final measurement. For absolute accuracy, use templates rather than rotary cutting, just as you would if you were hand-making the block.

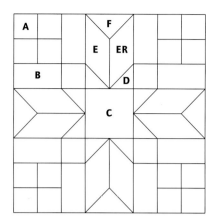

Figure 4.36

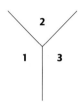

Figure 4.37

Hand Work

To hand piece the *Blackford's Beauty* block, lay out pieces **A**–**F** to match the drawing (fig. 4.36). Pin each step, right sides together, matching the marked seamlines. Stitch point to point, carefully following the seamlines.

This project introduces setting in a piece between two other pieces. It is done by stitching what is known as a Y-seam. Think of the three pieces as a unit (fig. 4.37).

The first seam sewn is the left arm of the Y. Join **1** and **2**.

The second seam sewn is the right arm of the Y. Join **2** and **3**.

The last seam sewn is the leg of the Y (fig. 4.38). Join **1** and **3**. It helps to fold Piece 2 in half, right sides together, just to move it out of the way.

This technique is very straightforward for hand stitching, since you are always stitching point to point.

1. Join one light **A** square to one dark **A** square. Repeat seven times. Join two pairs of **A** squares, always stitching a light **A** to a dark **A**. Repeat three times.
2. Join one dark **A** square to the end of one **B** rectangle. Repeat three times. Join one **B** rectangle to one **AA** unit. Repeat three times. Carefully noting the position of the dark **A** square, join one **AB** unit to one **AA-B** unit. Repeat three times.
3. Join two **E** parallelograms to one **F** triangle, using the Y-seam technique. Repeat three times. Join one **D** triangle to the end of each **E**.
4. Stitch rows as shown (fig. 4.39).

    Rows **1** and **3**: **AA–BA–B** to **DEF** to **AA–BA–B**

    (Watch rectangle and star point positions!)

    Row **2**: **DEF** to **C** to **DEF**
5. Join Rows **1** and **2**. Add Row **3**. Press carefully.

This block measures 12½″ (33.5cm) square, unfinished.

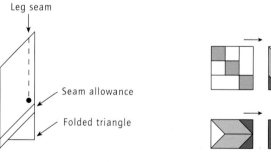

Figure 4.38   Figure 4.39

Machine Work

Sections of this block can be assembly line pieced. Setting-in must be done unit by unit.

1. Right sides together and using a ¼" (0.75cm) seam, sew one background strip and one chain strip together along one long cut edge. Repeat. Press the seams carefully toward the dark from both sides—first the back, then the front.

2. Recut across all strip sets at 2" (5.5cm) intervals for a total of 40 pairs.

3. Placing one pair, right sides together on another pair, matching seams and a dark to a light, chain-piece the pairs into 20 units (fig. 4.40). Press.

4. Recut the remaining 2" (5.5cm) background strips into (36) 2" × 3½" (5.5cm × 9.5cm) rectangles. Recut the remaining chain strips into four 2" × 3½" (5.5cm × 9.5cm) rectangles and sixteen 2" (5.5cm) squares.

   Right sides together, chain-piece one background rectangle to each corner square unit, as shown, for a total of 16 units. Press the seam toward the rectangle.

   Right sides together, chain-piece 16 chain squares to the end of 16 background rectangles. Finger press the seam toward the rectangle. Add these to the 16 corner square units (fig. 4.41).

5. Cut the extended star points from the 2" (5.5cm) strips using the **E–ER** template. Fold the strip in half, right sides together. Place the template on the strip and carefully cut the end angles. This automatically makes a pair of **E** pieces.

   Mark the "joint points" for the star points unit, as shown (fig. 4.42). Since there are no marks on the pieces when they are rotary cut, and since pieces that are joined in a Y-seam cannot have one seam oversewn by another, joint point marks are needed. These show where to begin and/or end a seam. Carefully make a hole in your template where the seams intersect and mark the fabric pieces with a pencil. Or using the small transparent ruler, place the ¼" (0.75cm) line on the cut edges of the fabric and draw two intersecting lines. The lines meet at the joint point. See also Appendix 2 on page 126.

   Join two extended star points to one background triangle (fig. 4.42), using the Y-seam technique shown on page 52. Pin the pieces, matching the marks. Stitch from the edge of the unit toward the joint point and backstitch. Repeat, for a total of 16 units.

   Add one small star point triangle to the end of each parallelogram, as shown (fig. 4.42).

6. Carefully noting the position of the corner units and star point units, chain together the following sequence: **AB** and **DEF**, **DEF** and **C**, **AB** and **DEF**, as shown (fig. 4.43). Open each unit. Chain on, in this order: **AB**, **DEF**, and **AB**, as shown (fig. 4.43).

7. Rotate the block one-quarter turn to the right. Right sides together, turn Row **1** over Row **2**, matching seams and turning Step 6 seams toward the corner and center units. Pin as necessary. Stitch edge to edge.

   Rotate the block 180°. Turn Row **3** over Row **2**, matching seams and turning Step 6 seams toward the corner and center units. Pin as necessary. Stitch edge to edge. Repeat Steps 6 and 7 for a total of four blocks.

This block measures 12½" (33.5cm) square, unfinished.

Figure 4.40

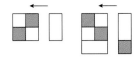

Figure 4.41

Joint points

Figure 4.42

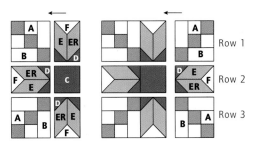

Figure 4.43

Setting

1. Arrange your blocks as in the quilt photo.
2. If not already pieced, stitch four **AA** corner units. Stitch one light **B** to one dark **B** on the long side. Repeat three times.
3. Measure the blocks to determine the length of the sashing strips. Cut the $3\frac{1}{2}''$ (9.5cm) sashing strips into 12 of these lengths.

   Stitch a sashing strip vertically between each pair of blocks, keeping the blocks on top as you work. Finish the rows by stitching a sashing strip vertically to each end. Press seams toward sashing strips.

   Make three rows of sashing strips and cornerstones, as shown. Note that the center strip is different from the other two. Press seams toward sashing strips.

   Join the block rows to the sashing and cornerstone rows, matching seams. Seams should fit well as they have been pressed in opposite directions. Press the assembled blocks.
4. Measure and cut the two side border pieces:

   _____ (length of side) $\times$ $3\frac{1}{2}''$ (9.5cm) wide

   Join assembled blocks to side borders. Pin and stitch, right sides together. Press seams toward the borders.

   Measure and cut the remaining two borders.

   _____ (length of side, including width of attached side borders) $\times$ $3\frac{1}{2}''$ (9.5cm) wide

   Join assembled top to remaining borders. Press seams toward the borders.

Backing, Quilting, and Binding

Make the quilt backing to measure 43" (120cm) square.

Prepare the quilt by basting the layers together. Again, as in Project 9, this is a block that probably needs quilting more to hold it in place than to embellish it. Consider using in-the-ditch or at the quarter inch quilting in these areas and 45° overlapping lines in the sashing and borders. You might also choose to quilt a straight line from corner to corner through the chain squares. The lines will form an X in the center of the stars. Then create radiating lines of stitching that follow the outside edges of the chain blocks and the V of the extended star points. These lines can be carried from the block through the sashing and border.

Make $4\frac{1}{2}$ yards (4.1m) of binding for your _Blackford's Beauty_ quilt.

Parallelograms add intrigue to many block patterns. They are different from 45° diamonds as they have two long and two short sides. Try _Windblown Square_, _Michigan Beauty_, _Union Star_, and _Memory_. You will also find blocks depicting flowers and baskets that use this shape, and border treatments using it to create chevrons. Add this interesting shape to your quiltmaking repertoire.

LeMoyne Star

45" × 60" (113cm × 150cm); 6 star blocks; sashing with cornerstones; 1 plain border

Mary Lynn Liebenow, Holmdel, New Jersey ◆ machine pieced; machine quilted

Color Clues—Using Stripes to Create Variety

Fascinating, eye-catching stripes seem to come and go in the fabric world. Therefore, when you see one that appeals to you, purchase it! You probably won't find it again. Each of the stars in this quilt appears to be different, although all are cut from the same fabric. A particular area of the stripe is selected and repeated for each diamond in the star. Enough yardage is critical here as you must use the same motif, in exactly the same position, eight times for each star. To maintain accuracy, each diamond must be cut separately as shown in the photograph.

To help repeat the design placement accurately, mark three registrations in pencil on your transparent template. Simply trace a key line or shape from the motif at the top, middle, and bottom of the template (fig. 4.45). Match these registration marks to the fabric when cutting out each diamond. Then erase these marks and draw new ones for the next star.

This technique can also be used with any patterned fabric that has sufficient variety and size in its motifs. You may hear this called "fussy cutting." Two small mirrors, set on their edges at a 45° angle to each other and placed on the fabric in this way, allow you to see what pattern repetitions are possible, and what these will look like when sewn together. Here are two additional stars, each made from stripes. These give the star an entirely different look.

Look for other ways that patterned stripes can be used to advantage in your quilts—in sashing and borders, as well as the blocks. Enjoy their creative potential!

Template with registration marks

Figure 4.45

Fabric Requirements

Stripe	2 yds. (2m)
Block background	¾ yd. (0.7m)
Sashing	¾ yd. (0.7m)
Border	1⅞ yds. (1.7m)
Backing	2¼ yds. (2.3m)
Binding	½ yd. (0.5m)
Batting	45″ × 60″ (114cm × 152cm)

Cutting with Hand Work Templates

For each block as shown, mark and cut:

	Template	Quantity
Identical star points	**A**	8
Background squares	**B**	4
Background triangles	**C**	4

Rotary Cutting for Machine Piecing Based on 42″ (106cm) selvage to selvage

	Quantity	Size
From striped fabric, cut	6 sets of 8	Template **A** diamonds
From block background, cut	3 strips	4″ (10.3cm)
recut strips into	*24 **B** squares*	*4″ (10.3cm)*
	6 squares	6¼″ (16.1cm)
*recut these squares twice on the diagonal to yield 4 triangles, for a total of 24 **C***		
for cornerstones	1 strip	3½″ (9cm)
recut strip into	*12 squares*	*3½″ (9cm)*
From sashing fabric, cut	6 strips	3½″ (9cm)
From border fabric, cut	4 strips, lengthwise	6½″ (16.5cm)

The templates for this project are provided in inches only. If you are working in centimeters, your may need to adjust the seam allowances, using as narrow as a 0.5cm seam allowance for the template pieces, as necessary. If in doubt, when you match up rotary-cut pieces with template-cut pieces prior to sewing, always use the rotary cut piece as a guide to final measurement. For absolute accuracy, use templates rather than rotary cutting, just as you would if you were hand-making the block.

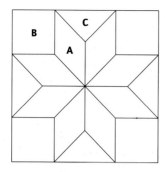

Figure 4.46

Sometimes a small hole remains in the center of the star (hard to imagine, but possible despite accurate cutting and stitching). To alleviate this, try running a single thread through the end point of each diamond. Insert the needle, carrying the thread through each point, moving around the "circle" until it returns to the point at which you started. Unthread the needle and pull up the two ends of the thread snugly, knotting them together. This will help to tighten up the center of the star.

Hand Work

To hand piece the *LeMoyne Star* block, lay out pieces **A**, **B**, and **C** to match the drawing (fig. 4.46). Pin each step, right sides together, matching the marked seamlines. Stitch point to point, carefully following the seamlines.

1. Join two **A** star points to one **B** square, using the technique for Y-seams (fig. 4.47). Repeat three times.
2. Join two **ABA** units to one **C** triangle, using the Y-seam technique. Repeat. This creates two halves of the block.
3. Join the two halves together by setting in the remaining **C** triangles, using the Y-seam technique.
4. Press the block—**AB** seams toward **B**, **AC** seams toward **A**, and **AA** seams either clockwise or counterclockwise going around the block. Open the seams at the center of the star and "fan" them around the circle as shown (fig. 4.48). Remember that pressing directions are suggestions; you alone can determine how your block will lay flat and look best.

This block measures 12½″ (31.5cm) square, unfinished.

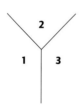

Figure 4.47

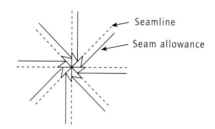

Figure 4.48

Machine Work

To machine piece one *LeMoyne Star* block, lay out pieces **A**, **B**, and **C** to match the drawing (fig. 4.46). Pin each step, right sides together, matching cut edges and marked joint points.

1. Mark the joint points on all **A**, **B**, and **C** pieces, as shown (fig. 4.49). The circled intersections must be marked.

2. Join two **A** star points to one **B** square, using the Y-seam technique. Stitch from the cut edge (the outer edge of the block or the center of the star) toward the joint point (fig. 4.50). Backstitch when reaching this point. Repeat three times.

3. Join two **ABA** units to one **C** triangle, using the Y-seam technique (fig. 4.51). Repeat.

4. Holding each unit with the **C** triangle at the top, finger press all **AA** seams to the right on both **ABA–C–ABA** units.

5. To join the **ABA–C–ABA** units, set in two **C** triangles, stitching just the right and left arms of the Y-seam (fig. 4.52a). This leaves the center of the block unstitched.

6. Right sides together, match and pin the center seam of the star. Because the star seams on each half are all pressed in the same direction, they should fit neatly together in the center. Fold the triangles at the ends of this seam, right sides together, with the Y arm seams pushed toward the triangles as shown (fig. 4.52b). Stitch the center seam. Open the center seam and press flat.

This block measures 12½″ (31.5cm) square, unfinished.

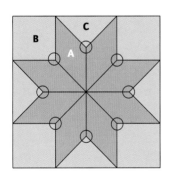

Figure 4.49

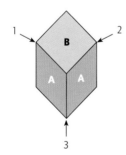

Figure 4.50

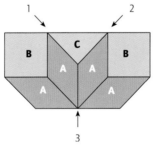

Figure 4.51

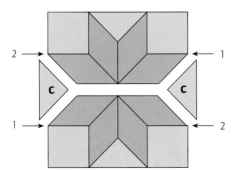

Figure 4.52a

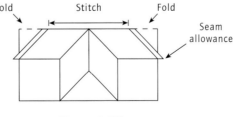

Figure 4.52b

Setting

1. Arrange your star blocks as in the quilt photo.
2. Measure the blocks to determine the length of the sashing strips. Cut the $3\frac{1}{2}$" (9cm) sashing strips into 17 of these lengths.
3. Stitch a sashing strip vertically between each pair of blocks. Finish the rows by stitching a sashing strip to each end. Press seams toward sashing strips.
4. Make four rows of sashing strips and cornerstones, as shown (fig. 4.52c). Press seams toward the sashing strips.
5. Join the block rows to the sashing and cornerstone rows, matching seams. Seams should fit well as they are pressed in opposite directions. Press the assembled blocks.
6. Measure and cut the two side border pieces:

   _____ (length of side) $\times$ $6\frac{1}{2}$" wide (16.5cm)

   Join assembled blocks to side borders. Pin and stitch, right sides together. Press seams toward the borders.
7. Measure and cut the remaining two borders:

   _____ (length of side, including width of attached side borders) $\times$ $6\frac{1}{2}$" (16.5cm) wide

   Join assembled top to remaining borders. Press seams toward the borders.

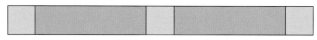

Figure 4.52c

Backing, Quilting, and Binding

Make the quilt backing to measure 49" $\times$ 64" (125cm $\times$ 163cm). The backing will have to be pieced on one side.

Prepare the quilt by basting the layers together. To best show off the clever patterns that you have created in the stars, use in-the-ditch quilting or quilting at $\frac{1}{4}$" (0.75cm). Save quilting motifs for the sashing, cornerstones, and borders, where they can be seen and appreciated. These areas can be filled with eight-pointed stars or cables, vines, swags, pumpkin seeds (a real pattern), overlapping circles—any number of linear patterns. Perhaps a motif from the striped fabric would make a good quilting pattern.

Make 6 yards (5.5m) of binding for your *LeMoyne Star* quilt.

Many blocks are based on the eight-pointed star. As you become more proficient, you may want to give some of them a whirl! Not all of the designs are stars or look like stars, however. Some of these different blocks are *Spider's Web*, *Flying Swallows*, *Enigma*, and *Castle Wall*. No doubt you will enjoy the great variety of these patterns.

Tumbling Blocks

39" × 40" (99cm × 102cm); 39 units; setting pieces; 2 plain mitered borders

Mary Lynn Liebenow, Holmdel, New Jersey ◆ machine pieced; machine quilted

Color Clues

This quilt pattern appeared in the 1850s and has been given many names, such as *Baby Blocks, Building Blocks,* and *Cubes and Stars.* It is a good choice for our discussion of relative value and depth. The dimensional effect of this pattern depends on the placement of light, medium, and dark fabrics.

To create the illusion of dimension on a flat surface, artists use value. If you look at a stack of real blocks on a table, light illuminates them from a source such as a window or lamp. The blocks then have a distinct light side (where the light shines most) and a dark or shadowed side (where the light doesn't reach). The third side appears less light than the first, yet not as dark as the other side. Translated into value, the blocks have a light side, a dark side, and a medium side. These values also give the impression of dimension (or depth) to the viewer.

You may decide to make this pattern from just three fabrics—light, medium, and dark. You may also select a wider range of fabrics, as shown in the sample quilt. If you look closely, you will see that the same fabric appears in a different place in different blocks. Its value depends on the fabrics with which it interacts. Therefore, while appearing light in one place, it may "read" as medium or even dark in another. Note what happens to the values of your fabrics as you add lighter and darker fabrics to the mix.

Using fabrics that feature motifs and colors of past eras adds another facet to your quiltmaking. You may be drawn to 1930s prints or shirting fabrics from the turn of the (last) century. Enjoy incorporating them into quilts using block styles of the period or using them to add a fresh twist to more contemporary designs. A cautionary note: Many collections seem to produce fabrics that are close in value. To enhance the vitality of your quilt, look beyond the collection and add supporting fabrics to extend the value range.

Fabric changes value depending on neighboring fabrics.

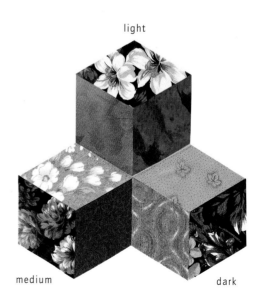

Fabric Requirements

For blocks	½ yd. (0.5m) *each*—lights, mediums, darks
Background	⅜ yd. (0.3m)
Inside border	¼ yd. (0.3m), cut crosswise
Outside border	1⅜ yds. (1.3m), cut lengthwise
Backing	1¼ yds. (1.3m)
Binding	½ yd. (0.5m)
Batting	45″ × 60″ (114cm × 152cm)

Cutting with Hand Work Templates

For the entire quilt, cut:

	Template	Quantity
Light, medium, and dark (each)	**A**	39
Background	**B**	4
Background	**C**	10
Background	**D**	6

Rotary Cutting for Machine Piecing Based on 42″ (106cm) selvage to selvage

From each light, medium, and dark fabric, cut one 2″ (5cm) strip. Open out the strip and place it across the mat. Cut the end of the strip at a 60° angle (fig. 4.53). Place the 60° angle line of the ruler on the cut edge of the strip nearest you and cut along the edge of the ruler, which you have moved as close as possible to the end of the strip. Keeping the 60° line at the cut edge, move the ruler to place the 2″ (5cm) line at the angle-cut end, and then cut across the strip along the edge of the ruler. Continue to cut the strip into 2″ (5cm) diamond pieces. Repeat for other strips and a total of 39 each—light, medium, dark.

From background fabric, cut one 2″ (5cm) strip. Open the strip and, using a machine-piecing template **D**, cut six.

From background fabric, cut two 1″ (2.5cm) strips. Open the strip and, using machine-piecing templates **C** and **B**, cut ten **C** and four **B**. To use the strip fabrics efficiently, turn the long side of the templates back and forth from one long cut edge to the other as you cut (see fig. 4.54).

For inner border, cut four 1½″ (3.8cm) strips, crosswise. For outer border, cut four 5½″ (14cm) strips, lengthwise (width of strip may be based on width of stripe used in the border).

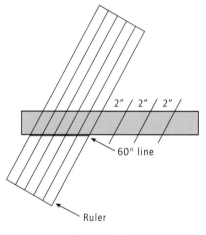

2″ 2″ 2″

60° line

Ruler

Figure 4.53

The templates for this project are provided in inches only. If you are working in centimeters, your may need to adjust the seam allowances, using as narrow as a 0.5cm seam allowance for the template pieces, as necessary. If in doubt, when you match up rotary-cut pieces with template-cut pieces prior to sewing, always use the rotary cut piece as a guide to final measurement. For absolute accuracy, use templates rather than rotary cutting, just as you would if you were hand-making the block.

D   D   D

Figure 4.54

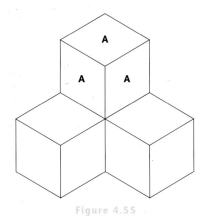

Figure 4.55

Hand Work

This project and the two additional quilts are interesting, not only for their patterns, but also for the way in which they go together. Here you will find units that are stitched together in rows, with setting shapes derived from the unit. All of these patterns are based on a 60° angle, and will provide lots of opportunity to use the Y-seam technique. Mark and cut accurately, stitch from point to point, and fine results will be yours!

Assemble each of the *Tumbling Block* units using the Y-seam technique (fig. 4.56). Be consistent in placing the light, medium, and dark fabrics. The sample quilt places the light in Position **2**, the medium in Position **1**, and the dark in Position **3**. You may change this; just do all of the units identically. All of these pieces are cut from template **A** and there are a total of 39 units.

Press the **1–2** seam toward **1**, the **2–3** seam toward **3**, and the **1–3** seam toward **3** (just tuck its top end under the **2–3** seam).

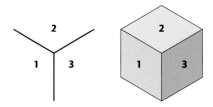

Figure 4.56

Texas Star

37" × 38" (94cm × 97cm);
8 complete blocks, 2 half blocks, setting triangles, 1 plain border

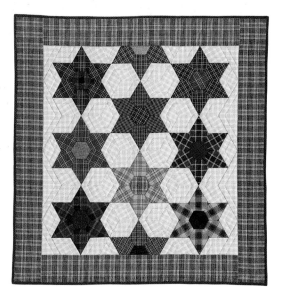

Janice B. Byrne, Atlantic Highlands, New Jersey ◆ machine pieced; machine quilted

A variation of the 60° shapes, this pattern uses kite shapes, hexagons, and diamonds. (See templates on page 144.)

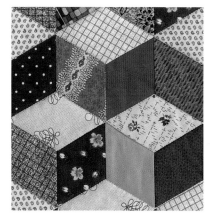

Machine Work

For every unit, mark all joint points. Because all pieces in this project are connected by Y-seams, you need to know where each seam begins and ends. A ¼″ (0.75cm) foot will be most helpful here, as it allows you to see the ¼″ (0.75cm) seam on both sides of the needle. You can then take a few stitches up to a point, put the needle down and lift the presser foot, turn the seam around and sew to the other point, and backstitch. Pin each seam carefully and keep a consistent ¼″ (0.75cm) seam.

For every unit, sew **A1** to **A2**, **A2** to **A3**, and **A1** to **A3**, in that order (fig. 4.57).

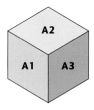

Figure 4.57

Inner City and Thousand Pyramids

40″ × 39″ (102cm × 99 cm);
3 *Inner City* blocks, 4 rows of pyramids, setting triangles, 1 plain border with appliqué

Mary Lynn Liebenow, Holmdel, New Jersey ◆ machine pieced and appliquéd; machine quilted

Try combining shapes based on the same angle. Consider a touch of appliqué for the border of a pieced quilt. These flowers enhance the triangle and half-hexagon shapes. Note how their shape is repeated in the quilting. (See templates on page 144.)

Setting

Lay out the units and the setting pieces. Work across the quilt from the top left, approaching each step as a Y-seam, so you are working with only three pieces at a time (fig. 4.58).

Row 1
Row 2
Row 3
Row 4
Row 5
Row 6
Row 7

Figure 4.58

1. Row **1**: Add corner triangle to **1**, as shown. Join setting triangle to **1** and **2**. The Y-seam is highlighted. Join setting triangle to **2** and **3**. Continue for a total of five Y-seams. Add corner triangle to **6**.
2. Row **2**: Join a side half-hexagon to **1** and **7**. Join **7**, **2**, and **8**. Continue down row, adding a half-hexagon in the last Y-seam. This row has six Y-seams.
3. Continue for Rows **3**, **4**, **5**, and **6**. When joining Row **7** to Row **6**, stitch the leg of the Y-seams only halfway and stop—don't backstitch.
4. Rotate quilt 180° so that Row **7** is in Row **1** position. Join corner triangle. Join the setting triangles as in Row **1**, finishing the leg seams of Row **7**. Press carefully.
5. Measure and cut the two side borders. Because these borders will be mitered, add more to the length:

   _____ (length of side + width of top and bottom border + 3″ [7.7cm])

   Inside border is cut 1½″ wide (3.8cm).
   Outside border is cut 5½″ wide (14cm) to accommodate the size of the stripe. If using a stripe, cut your border width based on the width of the stripe.
6. Measure and cut the two borders for the remaining two sides:

   _____ (length of side + width of side borders + 3″ [7.7cm])

7. Stitch each inside border piece to the corresponding outside border piece along one long cut edge. Press seams toward outside border for the sides. Press seams toward inside border for the top and bottom.
8. Pin the top border to the assembled blocks, remembering to measure and mark centers and the ¼″ (0.75cm) at each end of the seam. Stitch from the ¼″ (0.75cm) mark at one end of the seam to the ¼″ (0.75cm) mark at the other end; backstitch. Repeat for the remaining three borders.
9. Miter each corner, matching seams (see fig. 6.21–6.24 on page 100).

Backing, Quilting, and Binding

Make the quilt backing to measure 44″ (112cm) square.

Prepare the quilt by basting the layers together. Stitch in-the-ditch or quilt around each diamond at the ¼″ (0.75cm). Don't forget to quilt in the setting pieces as well. Stitch in-the-ditch on both sides of the inner border.

Make 4 yards (3.7m) of binding for your *Tumbling Blocks* quilt.

Setting in a shape is a great skill to master—congratulations! It will serve you well in other patterns. You might enjoy making a Grandmother's Flower Garden from hexagons and diamond shapes, or a quilt filled with six-pointed stars. Combinations of 60° shapes create striking patterns—as you will see in the additional two quilts.

Drunkard's Path

40" × 50" (102cm × 127cm); 48 blocks; 1 plain border with 4 corner blocks

Trish (Patti) Lenz, Cinebar, Washington ◆ Assembled by Katherine Kough ◆ machine pieced; machine quilted

Contrast achieved with pattern
scale and solids

Color Clues—Using Solids or Directionals

Working with solid-colored fabrics is both a joy and a challenge. The lack of printed motifs makes color and value placement more visually striking. Solids also offer a wonderful background for lots of quilting as there is no competition from printed patterns. While some quilters shy away from solids, I urge you to include them in your fabric collection. Buy as many colors in as many value steps as you can. They will be most valuable to use with printed fabrics, as well as standing alone in solid-tary (!) splendor.

Whether cut with great precision or off-grain serendipity, plaids and checks add charm to our quilts. These designs may be woven or printed. They are available in an astounding array of colors, values, and styles. But again, keep your eyes open and collect them when you see them. As with stripes, it could be a once-in-a-lifetime opportunity!

The fact that solids and directionals are so visually different from prints should be reason enough for their inclusion in our quilts. There is also strong historical precedent for their use. Consider the glorious Amish quilts, all stitched with solid fabrics, and the scrap quilts of the late 1800s, filled with directionals and prints of all sorts. Take the opportunity to enrich your own quiltmaking tradition by using these fabrics.

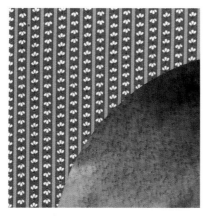

Fabric Requirements

Light and dark green	¼ yd. (0.3m)
Dark purple	¼ yd. (0.3m)
Light and dark pink	¼ yd. (0.3m)
Light and dark yellow	¼ yd. (0.3m)
Light and dark blue	¼ yd. (0.3m)
Light purple	⅜ yd. (0.3m)
Border	¾ yd. (0.7m)
Backing	1½ yds. (1.5m)
Binding	¾ yd. (0.7m)
Batting	45″ × 60″ (114cm × 152cm)

Cutting with Hand Work Templates

Mark and cut:

Template	Quantity
A	7 dark green, 8 dark purple, 7 dark pink, 3 dark yellow, 3 dark blue
B	7 light green, 8 light purple, 7 light pink, 3 light yellow, 3 light blue
C	4 light green, 2 light purple, 4 light pink, 7 light yellow, 7 light blue
D	4 dark green, 2 dark purple, 4 dark pink, 7 dark yellow, 7 dark blue

Rotary Cutting for Machine Piecing Based on 42″ (106cm) selvage to selvage

Cut one 5½″ (14cm) strip from each:

Light and dark green
Dark purple
Light and dark pink
Light and dark yellow
Light and dark blue

Cut two 5½″ (14cm) strips from light purple.

Use machine-piecing templates, placed on the strips, to cut the pieces listed under hand work templates.

Cut four 5½″ (14cm) strips from the border fabric.

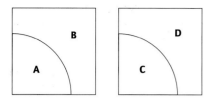

Figure 4.59

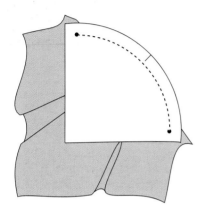

Figure 4.60a

Hand Work

To hand piece the *Drunkard's Path* block, lay out pieces **A**, **B**, **C**, and **D** to match the drawing (fig. 4.59). Pin the curve, right sides together, matching the center mark and the marked seamlines (fig. 4.60a). Stitch point to point, carefully following the seamlines.

An alternative way to approach a curved seam is to stitch from the center point to each end. Use an unknotted single thread. Begin at the center point, leaving half the thread hanging from the first stitch (fig. 4.60b). Sew to one end of the curve and knot the thread. Unthread the needle and rethread it with the remaining thread. Sew to the other end of the curve and knot the thread. The curve in these templates is quite gentle and easy to pin. This method is especially valuable with a deeper curve, requiring pinning on only half of the curve at one time.

Stitch **A–B** and **C–D** combinations:

    A–B 7 green, 8 purple, 7 pink, 3 yellow, 3 blue
    C–D 4 green, 2 purple, 4 pink, 7 yellow, 7 blue

This block measures 5½" (14cm) square, unfinished.

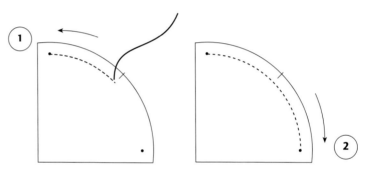

Figure 4.60b

Machine Work

Pin and stitch each curve. Use three pins—one in the center, one near each end. Often it is easiest to stitch a curve with the convex (fat, outer curve) piece next to the machine feed dogs and the concave (thin, inner curve) piece on top. The piece that needs to be eased is then against the feed dogs and the piece that stretches slightly is on top in clear view.

Make the block combinations as listed in the hand work section. Because this is such a gentle curve, you can carefully press the curved seam toward the darker fabric, with either shape.

This block measures 5½" (14cm) square, unfinished.

Setting

1. Arrange your blocks as in the quilt photo.
2. Stitch the blocks together in rows and join the rows, matching seam intersections.
3. Measure and cut the two side borders:

   _____ (length of side) $\times$ 5½″ (14cm) wide

   Join assembled blocks to side borders. Pin and stitch, right sides together. Press seams toward the borders.
4. Measure and cut the remaining two borders:

   _____ (length of blocks *only*, plus seam allowance) $\times$ 5½″ (14cm) wide

   Add a block (watch placement) to each end of the two borders. Press seams toward border pieces. Join assembled top to remaining borders, matching seam intersections. Pin and stitch, right sides together. Press seams toward borders.

Backing, Quilting, and Binding

Make the quilt backing to measure 44″ $\times$ 54″ (112cm $\times$ 137cm).

Prepare the quilt by basting the layers together. Hold the blocks in place by stitching in-the-ditch. The sample quilt shows some long lines of quilting on the diagonals of the design. Also you will see pieced curves held in place with in-the-ditch quilting and curves repeated in decorative stitching lines.

For something different, you might consider big stitch hand quilting (a ¼″ [0.75cm] running stitch) with cotton or rayon embroidery floss on this project. Large stitches in bright or contrasting colors are very effective against the solid fabrics.

Make 5¼ yards (4.8m) of binding for your *Drunkard's Path* quilt.

Learning to stitch curved seams allows you access to another whole category of quilt block designs. Their interpretation can range from very traditional to highly contemporary. Try some of these designs to practice your curved piecing skills: *Orange Peel*, *Mill Wheel*, *Robbing Peter to Pay Paul*, and *Hearts and Gizzards*. Have fun!

Chrysanthemum and Fans

34″ × 34″ (86cm × 86cm); 4 blocks; 20 border blocks; 1 plain border

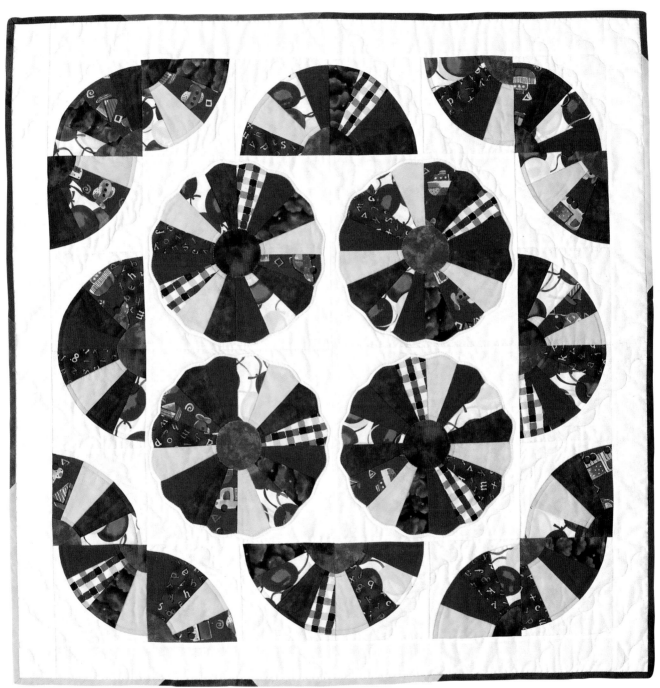

Barbara F. Caffrey, Sebastian, Florida ◆ machine pieced and appliquéd; machine quilted

Color Clues—Using Triads

Many color schemes can be created by choosing three colors equidistant from each other on a color circle. Or think of it this way—select a color, skip three colors, use the next color, skip three colors, use the next color. The same thing will happen if you place an equilateral (60°) triangle on the circle and look at the colors touched by the three points.

The sample quilt is based on the primary triad of red, yellow, and blue. Touches of the secondary triad—green, orange, and violet—have also been used. This is a bright, happy, and busy quilt!

If you seek to expand your range of color schemes, try using a combination of red-orange, yellow-green, and blue-violet, or yellow-orange, red-violet, and blue-green. These are unusual and challenging—probably most comfortably used in subtle shades or tints, although there are dynamite fabrics that feature them in full-blown saturated color.

Here are three fan blocks illustrating triadic color combinations. Make a paper triangle, drop it on a color circle, and see what happens. Try using some new, vibrant triad-based fabrics in your quilts, and you'll discover the versatility of the triadic color harmony.

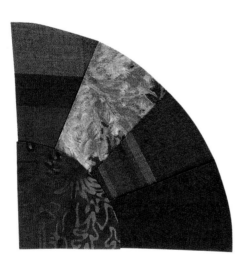
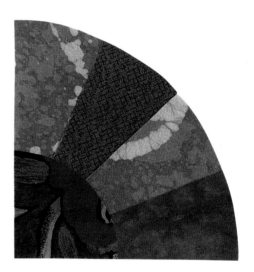
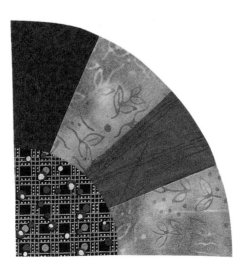

Fabric Requirements

Background	1½ yds. (1.5m)
Nine fabrics (includes binding)	¼ yd. each (0.3m)
Backing	1⅛ yds. (1.1m)
Batting	45″ × 60″ (114cm × 152cm)
Nonwoven sew-in lightweight interfacing	1 yd. (1m) (machine piecing only)

Cutting with Hand Work Templates

	Template/Size	Quantity
For each *Chrysanthemum* block, mark and cut		
petals	**A**	16
center	**B**	1
Background	12″ × 12″ (30cm × 30cm)	1
For each *Fan* border block, mark and cut		
fan blades	**C**	4
center	**D**	1
Background	5½″ × 5½″ (14.5cm × 14.5cm)	1

Rotary Cutting for Machine Piecing Based on 42″ (106cm) selvage to selvage

	Quantity	Size
From background fabric, cut	4	12″ × 12″ (30cm × 30cm)
	3	5½″ (14.5cm) strips
recut 3 strips into	20	5½″ (14.5cm) squares
	4	2½″ (6.5cm) strips for border
From nine fabrics, cut a total of	64	petals **A**
	80	fan blades **C**
	4	circle centers **B**
	20	quarter-circle centers **D**
From interfacing, cut	4	11″ squares (28cm)
Border fabric	4	2½″ (6.5cm) strips

Use a machine-piecing template to cut the petals and blades. Remember, you may use the hand-piecing template to create the machine-piecing template by adding ¼″ (0.75cm) seam allowance on all sides. Be careful not to shave any edges off the template with the rotary cutter. It is easier to cut the centers by marking them and using scissors.

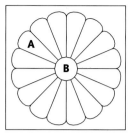

Figure 4.61

Figure 4.62

Figure 4.63

Figure 4.64

Hand Work

Cutting accurate templates and pieces is especially important for this block. Petals that are too wide or too narrow will not make a circle that lays flat.

To hand piece the *Chrysanthemum* block, lay out 16 **A** petals in a circle (fig. 4.51), arranging the colors to your satisfaction. Pin each step, right sides together, matching the marked seamlines. Stitch point to point, carefully following the seamlines.

1. Stitch two **A** petals together along one long side. Repeat seven times to make eight pairs. Join two pairs of **A** petals together, as in Step 1. Repeat three times to make four 4-petal units.

2. Join two 4-petal units together, as in Step 1. Repeat. Join the 8-petal units together, as in Step 1. Press, taking care to not distort the circle.

3. Fold the block background square in half, twice, finger pressing the folds. Open the block and lay it flat, right side up (fig. 4.62). Place the flower right side up on the block, centering the petals and aligning every fourth petal seam with a fold line. Pin in place.

4. Turn under the curved seam allowance at the top of each petal, finger pressing it and pinning it to the background block. You may need to trim the seam allowances slightly to produce a smooth curve. Baste the edge of the center opening of the petals to the background block inside the ¼" (0.75cm) seam allowance. Stitch the tops of the petals to the background block using a blind stitch (refer to appliqué on page 79) or a very small running stitch through the seam allowance close to the edge of the petals.

5. To make a "perfect" circle for the center of the petals, cut the template circle **B** from poster board or heat-tolerant template plastic. Baste around the marked and cut fabric circle within the seam allowance. Place the template on the back of the circle, and draw up the ends of the basting thread, causing the seam allowance to fold over the template (fig. 4.63). Pull the thread to gather the seam allowance evenly over the template. Press the back and front of your fabric circle, producing a firm crease around the circle. Loosen the threads and pop out the template. Draw up the threads again, just enough to make the seam allowance lay flat. Knot and cut off the ends. Center, pin, and stitch the circle, matching your stitch selection to Step 5. Trim the block to 10½" (27.5cm) square, keeping the *Chrysanthemum* centered.

To hand stitch a *Fan* block, lay out four **C** fan blades next to each other, arranging the colors to your satisfaction.

1. Stitch two blades together along one long side. Repeat. Join the two pairs. Press.

2. Fold the background block in half diagonally and finger press the fold. Open the block, place the blades on a marked fold corner of the block (fig. 4.64), and pin the fan in place.

3. Turn under the seam allowance, finger press, and pin to the background block. Trim the seam if necessary to produce a smooth curve. Stitch the top of the blades in place, matching *Chrysanthemum* stitch selection.

4. Turn under the curved edge of the quarter-circle center **D**. Finger press and trim if necessary. Set the quarter-circle in place at the base of the fan, aligning the raw edges with the edge of the block. Pin and stitch. Baste the outside edges of the fan block to hold the blades in place.

Machine Work

Stitch these *Chrysanthemum* blocks with a little help from a dressmaking technique—a facing!

1. Right sides together and using a ¼" (0.75cm) seam, join two petals on one long side. Repeat seven times.
2. Join four pairs of petals, as in Step 1.
3. Join the two units of eight petals, as in Step 1. Press the seams counterclockwise around the center carefully; don't distort the circle.
4. Place the circle of 16 petals, right side down, on an 11" (28cm) square of interfacing. Pin.
5. Using a very small stitch length and a ¼" (0.75cm) seam, stitch around the tops of all the petals. To sew these curves, begin at the center of a petal and stitch to a seam. Stop with the needle down at this point, lift the presser foot slightly, and reposition the block so that you can stitch forward at the proper seam width. Repeat this *stop, pivot, start* at each seam (fig 4.65). When you return to the beginning of this seam, oversew a few of the stitches to lock the seam.

6. Very carefully trim the seam allowance of this outside edge to a scant ⅛" (0.3cm). Turn the *Chrysanthemum* right side out through the center opening. Gently roll the outside edge of the flower between your fingers to "press" it flat. Press, making sure that the lining doesn't show around the edges.
7. Fold the background block in half, twice, finger pressing the folds (fig. 4.66). Place the flower right side up on the block: center the petals and align every fourth petal seam with a fold line. Pin in place.
8. Using the technique in Step 6 under Hand Work, press the center circle. Pin in place.
9. Using a blind hemstitch, blanket stitch, straight stitch, or decorative embroidery stitch, sew the edges of the center circle and the flower petals to the background block. Going slowly will help you stitch evenly around the curves.

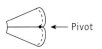

Figure 4.65   Figure 4.66

If you find that the background fabric is pulling up or "scrunching" in under the flower, use a piece of stabilizer, such as Tear Easy™, between the feed dogs and the block. Remove the stabilizer after sewing.

Trim the block to 10½" (27.5 cm) square, keeping the *Chrysanthemum* centered.

To machine piece a *Fan* block, lay out four **D** fan blades next to each other, arranging the colors to your satisfaction.

1. Right sides together and using a ¼" (0.75cm) seam, stitch two blades together along one long side. Repeat. Join the two pairs of blades, as above.
2. Complete the block, following Hand Work Steps 2 to 4, using the stitch selection as in Step 9 above.

Setting

1. Lay out your blocks as in the quilt photo or make your own border arrangement.
2. Join the four *Chrysanthemum* blocks.
3. Join four *Fan* blocks for the side border. Repeat. Pin and stitch the side borders to the assembled center blocks, matching seams. Join six *Fan* blocks for one remaining border. Repeat. Pin and stitch the remaining borders to the assembled top, matching seams.
4. Measure and cut the two side plain border pieces:

   _____ (length of side) $\times$ 2½″ (6.5cm) wide

   Join the assembled blocks to side plain borders. Pin and stitch. Press seams toward plain borders. Measure and cut the two remaining plain border pieces:

   _____ (length of side, including width of attached borders) $\times$ 2½″ (6.5cm) wide

   Join the assembled quilt top to the remaining plain border pieces. Pin and stitch. Press seams toward plain borders.

Backing, Quilting, and Binding

Make the backing to measure 38″ (97cm) square.

Prepare the quilt by basting the layers together. Because there are so many seams in these patterns and an extra layer of fabric under the flowers and fans, choose the placement of your quilting stitches wisely. The extra bulk doesn't present much of a problem for machine quilters, but it can make hand quilting difficult.

The project sample is quilted by machine at ¼″ (0.75cm) around the outside of the flower centers and the fan centers. It also has a ¼″ (0.75cm) line of stitching around the *outside* of the flowers. The fans are quilted at ¼″ (0.75cm) *inside* the top curve. Between the blocks and in the corners, Barbara has used an elongated machine embroidery stitch that mimics the arrangement of the corner *Fan* blocks. It is quite effective! The choice of transparent thread inside the blocks and white thread on the background is a good one because the fabrics are so bright and busy.

Make 4¼″ yards (4.1m) of binding for your *Chrysanthemum* and *Fans* quilt. This binding is different only because it is made of lots of colors. Cut the pieces for the binding from each of the nine fabrics used in the petals and fan blades. It provides a wonderful, whimsical touch to finish this happy quilt.

Many challenging block patterns are based on divisions of a circle. At one time, they were all extraordinarily difficult to piece, but with the advent of foundation paper piecing, some of them are achievable fairly early in your quilting career. If these intrigue you, look for the patterns at your local quilt shop or when you attend shows where vendors are present. Enjoy trying this method of piecework.

Chapter 5

Basic Appliqué Techniques

Having come this far, you won't be surprised to read that there are many ways to approach appliqué. All methods basically accomplish the same thing: fabric shapes are stitched into arrangements on a background fabric. These blocks are usually planned and drawn out first. Then the templates for the individual elements within the appliqué are made, and the layout of the block is transferred to the background. Let's consider three popular methods.

NEEDLETURN APPLIQUÉ

Most people think of appliqué in the traditional needle-turned manner: a shape is cut from one fabric and attached with a blind stitch to a second, larger piece of background fabric. These shapes may be free-cut or follow a pattern. The edge of the shape is turned under and stitched down in an almost invisible manner.

Some fabrics are not really suitable. Loosely woven fabrics should not be used for appliqué. The narrow seam allowances permit threads from the cut edge to escape. Polyester-cotton blends are also problematic, as their very nature prevents a sharply creased edge. One hundred percent cotton broadcloth fabrics usually produce the best results.

To use an appliqué template, trace around it on the right side of the fabric. Use a marking pencil that produces just enough line for you to see. Cut outside the drawn line, adding ⅛" to ³⁄₁₆" (0.3cm to 0.5cm). The difficulty in producing smooth lines and curves is caused by seam allowances that are too large.

To attach appliqués, finger press the seam allowance to the back of each shape before it is pinned or basted in place. This should put any drawn lines on the edge of the shape and make them virtually invisible. The placement of the appliqués can be as free or controlled as you wish. Appliqué is a very flexible medium. You may choose to mark the exact shapes of all the appliqués on the background block, just the center point for each piece, or only places where pieces meet or overlap.

It is even possible to put a drawing of the finished block on a light box and to place the background over the drawing to show where to pin the next piece. I prefer as few marks on the background as possible.

Select a thread that closely matches the color of the appliqué. Use a thin needle: I like John James Sharps (size 11 or 12) or EZ Gold Eye Appliqué Sharps (size 10). Invest in a good needle threader if you have mature eyes (and limited patience!) like yours truly. Thinner threads, such as machine embroidery thread or silk, make the task easier and facilitate almost invisible stitching. Cutting the thread at an angle before inserting it through the needle's eye or moistening the eye of the needle is also helpful. Thin needles really make a great difference in the ease of stitching. Use them!

Thread the needle with no more than 18″ (45cm) of thread, making a small knot at the end. Insert the needle and single thread into the back of the background fabric, under the edge of the appliqué. Bring the needle up through and out the edge of the appliqué (fig. 5.1).

The appliqué stitch is very simple:

1. Hold the needle parallel to the edge of the appliqué shape, with the point of the needle just at the spot where the thread exited (fig 5.2).
2. Slide the point of the needle under the edge of the appliqué, insert it into the background fabric, push it forward about ⅛″ to ³⁄₁₆″ (0.3cm to 0.5cm), and bring the point out at the edge of the appliqué once again (fig. 5.3).

Inserting the needle point directly under the edge of the appliqué where the last stitch exited permits the thread to roll right over the edge (fig. 5.4). This way, the least amount of thread is visible. On the back of the block, these stitches are slightly angled (fig. 5.5). End the thread by knotting it on the back of the block.

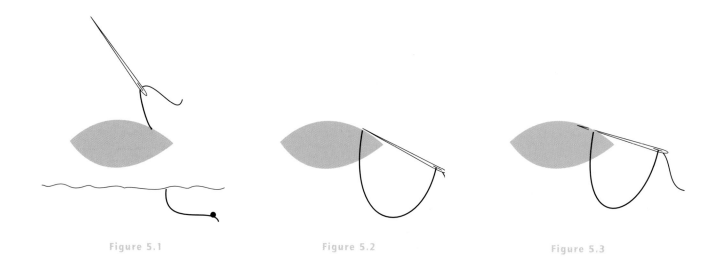

Figure 5.1   Figure 5.2   Figure 5.3

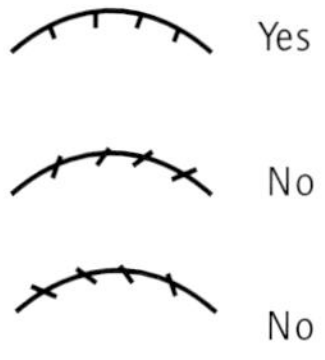

Yes

No

No

Figure 5.4    Figure 5.5

FREEZER PAPER APPLIQUÉ

Another way to approach appliqué is to use freezer paper for templates. This paper is most useful, because it can be ironed to the fabric and removed (multiple times if desired). Draw on the paper side; iron the waxy side to the fabric with medium heat. Again, there are several methods:

Method 1. Trace the shape and cut out the freezer paper template. Iron it to the *right* side of the fabric. Cut the seam allowance around it. Leave the paper in place and stitch around the appliqué shape, using the freezer paper as a guide. Gently peel off the paper.

Method 2. Trace the appliqué shape, *reversed*; cut out the freezer paper template. Iron it to the *wrong* side of the fabric. Cut the seam allowance around it. Finger press or iron the seam allowance to the back of the shape, using the freezer paper as a guide to achieve a nice sharp edge. Gently peel off the paper, pin the appliqué in place, and stitch.

Method 3. Cut out the freezer paper template. Pin or use a dab of water-soluble glue stick to hold the paper side to the *wrong* side of the fabric. Cut the seam allowance around it. Iron the seam allowance down onto the waxy side of the paper. Leave the paper in place and stitch around the edge, either by hand or by machine, using a narrow, elongated zigzag or a blind hemstitch (fig. 5.6). After stitching, carefully slit the background fabric behind the appliqué, and withdraw the paper. Many stitchers like this method because it stabilizes the edges of the appliqué shape.

Figure 5.6

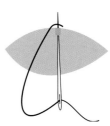

Figure 5.7a

Figure 5.7b

FUSED APPLIQUÉ

For ultimate stabilization, you may decide to fuse your appliqués. Trace the appliqué shapes, *reversed*, on the paper side of fusible webbing. Following the manufacturer's instructions, use an iron to bond the webbing side to the wrong side of the fabric (the iron is touching the paper side). Following the lines, cut out the shapes; gently peel off the paper. The shapes can now be bonded in place on the background fabric. See Appendix 2 for information about nonstick pressing sheets, must-have tools for working with fusibles.

The edges still must be stitched. Often a blanket stitch is used for hand sewing. Either a blanket stitch or a close-packed zigzag stitch called a satin stitch can be used when stitching by machine. Decorative or thicker threads may be used to achieve a particular look, such as folk art or "flashy trash."

To make the basic blanket stitch, bring the knotted thread up through the background, close to the edge of the appliqué. Insert the needle ³⁄₁₆″ to ¼″ (0.5cm to 0.75cm) inside the edge of the appliqué, going down through the appliqué and the background, bringing the needle out at the edge of the appliqué once again. The thread passes under the needle with each stitch (fig. 5.7a–b), creating a line of thread around the outside of the shape.

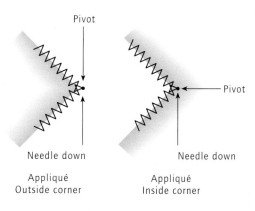

Figure 5.9

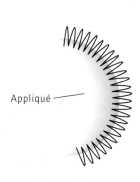

Figure 5.8

Satin stitching provides a definitive edge for appliqué shapes. Here are some tips to remember:

1. Test the width, length, and tension of the stitch before beginning work on the actual block.
2. Use a stabilizer, such as Tear-Easy™, between the block and the feed dogs to keep the background from puckering.
3. When stitching along curves, go slowly and remember to slightly overlap the stitches on the tighter side of the curve. This prevents the stitches from spreading apart on the wider side (fig. 5.8).
4. When turning corners, always stop with the needle down, lift the presser foot, and pivot. For an *outside* corner, the needle stops *outside* the appliqué; for an *inside* corner, stop *in* the appliqué (fig. 5.9).

Other decorative embroidery stitches, done by either hand or machine, can be used to edge or embellish appliqués. Remember these basic considerations:

- Use marking tools that do not leave permanent lines.
- Avoid loosely woven fabrics.
- Test fabric by pinching it to see if it creases sharply.
- Use a thin needle for hand stitching.
- Use color-compatible thread; fine, when possible, for hand appliqué.
- Keep the background flat as you stitch; don't let it draw up under the appliquéd pieces.

The following projects will give you ample opportunity to learn and practice all the basic shapes and seams used for appliqué. Each project is different to give you a taste of several styles. Enjoy!

Lagoon

32" × 32" (81cm × 81cm)

Joy Bohanan, Red Bank, New Jersey ◆ hand appliquéd; hand quilted

This wall hanging is designed to teach a number of basic needleturn appliqué techniques—the appliqué stitch, corners, points, curves, and stems—as well as some fun fancywork—stuffing, ruching, and layering. Choose to follow the sample, arrange the pieces in your own design, or put each element into a separate block, sewing them all together as a sampler quilt. Your fabric selections may be as realistic or fanciful as you please.

Fabric Requirements

Water	⅝ yd. (0.5m)
Fish	two 8″ (20cm) squares
Log	⅛ yd. (0.1m)
Turtle shell	one 6″ (15cm) square
Turtle	one 8″ (20cm) square
Coral	two 6″ × 14″ (15cm × 36cm) pieces
Starfish	one 8″ (20cm) square
Shells	five 8″ (20cm) squares
Bubbles	five 2″ (5cm) squares
Seaweed	three ⅛ yd. (0.1m)
Crab	one 10″ (2.5cm) square
Sky	¼ yd. (0.3m)
Lobster trap	¼ yd. (0.3m)
Backing	1 yd. (1m)
Border	⅝ yd. (0.6m)
Binding	½ yd. (0.5m)

Cutting

Cut

water	20½″ (52cm) square
sky	6½″ × 20½″ (16.5cm × 52cm)
bottom border	6½″ × 20½″ (16.5cm × 52cm)
side borders	6½″ × 32½″ (16.5cm × 83cm)

Hand Work

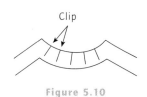

Clip

Figure 5.10

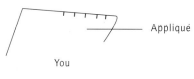

Background

Appliqué

You

Figure 5.11a

1. Mark the wave pattern onto the top of the water square. Cut the seam allowance at ³⁄₁₆″ (0.5cm). Clip, cutting into the seam allowance toward—but not touching—the marked seamline, along the curve at ⅜″ (0.5cm) intervals (fig. 5.10). Pin the top edge of the water square above the bottom edge of the sky.

2. Mark, cut out, and position the log. With the edge of the appliqué away from you, practice the appliqué stitch on these long edges (fig. 5.11a). Keep your stitches about ⅛″ (0.3cm) apart. Turn under and pin down the seam allowances of the water where it passes under the log. Where one appliqué covers another (e.g., log over water edge), you may elect not to stitch the underneath edge. It will be secured by the piece on top.

   To turn the corner when you reach the bump on the top of the log, stitch up to the corner and take another stitch very close to the last stitch (fig. 5.11b). This secures the corner. Using the tip of your needle, turn under the next seam allowance, snugging the end of it right up to the last stitches. Continue around the log, back to the edge of the water square.

3. Now, stitch down the edge of the water. Smooth the clipped curves gently with your needle as you work. The points here are slightly sharper than the corners on the log, but the principle is the same.

Figure 5.11b

4. The following is a method for making pieces to represent stems, basket strips, porch railings, or any linear item. In this case, it's a lobster trap. If the pieces need to curve, cut them on the bias; if they are to be stitched straight, they can be cut on the cross-grain. The width of the strip can be adjusted as needed. From the lobster trap fabric, cut two 1½″ (3.8cm) cross-grain strips and enough 1½″ (3.8cm) bias to equal 15″ (38cm) in length; seam pieces together if necessary. Fold all pieces in half lengthwise, wrong sides together, and press gently.

   a. Position the folded straight strips, cut to size, one at a time. The ends of these strips will be covered by the curved bias and the side border.

   b. Sew a small running stitch through both layers of "stem" and the background, a scant ⅛″ (0.3cm) from the center of the strip on the side of the raw edges (fig. 5.12). Secure the ends.

   c. Turn the folded edge up and over the raw edges and stitch in place with the appliqué stitch.

      The result is a full clean-edged piece. After all straight pieces are stitched, position and stitch the curved bias piece. Either tuck under and sew down the ends, or hide them under the shell and starfish.

5. Mark, cut out, and position the two coral pieces. Note that one piece overlaps the other; the base of both appliqués is secured in the bottom border seam. Stitch down **A**, with edge of **B** turned and pinned beneath. Leave open the indicated area for the insertion of the ruched seaweed piece. It will be stitched down later. Stitch down **B**, from the edge of **A** to the "leave open" mark. This seam will be finished after the side border is added.

6. Add the bottom border, right sides together, using a ¼″ (0.75cm) seam. Add the left side border. Add the right side border, leaving open a space to insert the ruched seaweed piece. Finish stitching down coral **B**.

7. Mark, cut out, and position the starfish. Work on producing smooth curves. At the tips (outer curves) of the starfish, clip small V shapes into the seam allowance (fig. 5.13). This allows the seam to turn under more compactly. Inner curves can be clipped with a straight cut, because the seam allowances spread out when turned.

Figure 5.12   Figure 5.13

8. Mark, cut out, and position one fish. Start to stitch on a long smooth side. Don't begin stitching appliqué pieces at a point or at the middle of an inside curve—it just makes the task unnecessarily difficult. To stitch sharp points, stop ½" (1.5cm) before reaching the point. Fold the seam allowance at the tip down and fold under the rest of the seam you are stitching (fig. 5.14a). Continue stitching to the tip, taking one slightly longer stitch straight off the tip and into the backing (fig. 5.14b). This helps to give the illusion of a longer, sharper tip. Trim any excess seam allowance from the tip or side that was turned under. Tuck under the last seam of the point.

   To stitch inside points, carefully clip to the V shape (fig. 5.14c). As you approach this point, begin making your stitches closer together (fig. 5.14d). Within a few stitches of the V and at the V, take deeper stitches onto the appliqué. Also do this at the V. This covers the exposed fabric threads on the edge of the appliqué with sewing threads. As you stitch out of the V, keep the first few stitches very close together, then gradually resume your normal pattern. Mark, cut out, position, and sew the second fish.

9. To make the circular bubbles, refer to directions on page 76, Step 5.

10. Mark, cut out, and position the turtle. Stitch the body of the turtle in place. Mark the turtle shell. Cut out around the outside edge and inside shapes, leaving a ³⁄₁₆" (0.5cm) seam allowance. Clip all curves in these shapes. Position and pin the shell on top of the turtle. Stitch it in place, using your needle point to gently smooth the inside curves as you work.

11. Mark and cut out the crab. Pin from the claw joint at the body around the legs to the other claw, allowing the body to puff up a bit. Stitch this part down first. Then pin down the claws and stitch them. Insert small bits of batting into the crab through the open area between the two claws. Don't overstuff; the background must remain flat. Stitch down the rest of the crab, adding two beads for eyes.

Note: You can change the look of the turtle shell by inserting pieces of different fabric into the shell openings before stitching everything down.

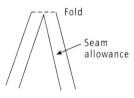

Figure 5.14a

Figure 5.14b

Figure 5.14c

Figure 5.14d

12. To ruche the seaweed, cut 1½" (1.5cm) wide straight strips—36", 20", and 15" (91cm, 51cm, and 38cm) long. Fold the long cut edges toward the center of each strip right side out, and press in place (fig. 5.15a). With a slightly larger needle and a single sturdy thread (knotted at the end), sew small running stitches along the strip at right angles to the edges. Here's the important part: at each folded edge, carry the thread *over the edge* and begin the running stitch from the other side (fig. 5.15b). It doesn't matter which side you begin each stitching line from, just be sure to carry the thread over the edge. When you pull up the thread, the strip will gather; stitching over the edge makes the wonderful texture. Stitch 6" to 8" (15cm to 20cm) and gather; repeat to the end of the strip. At the end that will not be concealed, tuck in the raw edges and sew the running stitch right over them. Position the seaweed and stitch securely in place, concealing the stitches in the folds. Stitch closed all openings left for the seaweed.

13. To layer the seashells, simply mark and cut out each layer. Position and stitch down in order, from bottom to top. This creates another three-dimensional look.

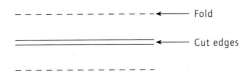

Fold

Cut edges

Figure 5.15a

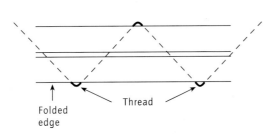

Thread

Folded edge

Figure 5.15b

Backing, Quilting, and Binding

Make a backing 40" (102cm) square.

Prepare the quilt by basting the layers together. Joy has hand quilted details into the individual elements of the scene, such as striations on the coral pieces and clouds in the sky. The water and border areas are quilted with circles and undulating lines, suggesting bubbles and water movement.

Make 3¾ yards (3.5m) of binding for your *Lagoon* quilt.

Enjoy using the appliqué skills learned and practiced here on Joy's delightful design. Choose colors and add touches to make it truly your own. You might also decide to fuse and stitch down all the flat shapes by machine. Whatever your approach, have fun!

Folk Flora

35" × 35" (88cm × 88cm); 4 blocks; sashing and border

Louise Haley, Mesa, Arizona ◆ machine appliquéd; machine quilted

Fabric Requirements

Background	1 yd. (1m)
Flowers, leaves, stems	¼ yd. (0.3m) *each* dark green, light green, dark red, bright red, dark blue, light blue, light gold, dark gold
Sashing, border	1 yd. (1m)
Backing	1⅛ yds. (1.1m)
Binding	½ yd. (0.5m)
Border	1⅛ yd. (1.1m)

Cutting

Cut four background blocks 13½″ (34cm) square. Often, appliqué stitchers like to cut background blocks larger, trimming them to size after the appliqué is completed. This alleviates concerns about distorting the square block during the appliqué process.

Sashing—cut 3½″ (9cm) strips
Border—cut 4½″ (11.5 cm) strips

Hand or Machine Work

This project lends itself equally well to hand or machine appliqué. The thin stems can be done by machine, using a zigzag or buttonhole stitch to hold the folded edge in place. Try pressing the pieces over freezer paper, then stitching with transparent thread and narrow, elongated zigzag stitches.

Block A—Cutwork Flower Spray

1. Cut 24″ (61cm) of 1″ (2.5cm) bias for stems. Position and stitch, as shown previously on page 85 (fig 5.12).
2. Mark, cut, position, and stitch center circle as shown on page 76 (fig. 4.63). Mark, cut, position and stitch eight leaves.
3. Mark, cut, position, and stitch four large flower pieces.
4. Mark, cut, position, and stitch five teardrop pieces for each flower.

The teardrop shapes may also be done as reverse appliqué, with additional fabric inserted under each shape, rather than placed on top. See directions in Step 10 of Project 11, *Lagoon*.

Trim block to 12½″ (31.5cm) square.

Block B—Oak Leaves and Acorns

1. Mark, cut, and position the center seed pods.
2. Mark, cut, position, and stitch four acorns. Remember, the top edge of the acorn does not have to be appliquéd, as it is covered by the seed pods.
3. Stitch the center seed pods.
4. Mark, cut, position, and stitch four oak leaves.

Trim block to 12½″ (31.5cm) square.

Learn to approach appliqué blocks as layers from the bottom to the top. You first stitch the elements that will be partially covered, working your way to the top pieces. Some stitchers trim out whatever fabric is underneath an appliqué; others do not. When a lighter fabric is placed over a darker fabric, some quilters line the lighter piece, rather than cut away the darker fabric. Yet another opportunity for you to experiment and choose the method that suits you best!

Block C—Layered Cabbage Rose

1. Mark, cut, and position largest petal circle **1**.
2. Mark, cut, position, and stitch four leaves, slipping base of leaves under petal circle. Stitch petal circle **1**.
3. Mark, cut, position, and stitch petal circles **2**, **3**, and **4**, in that order.
4. Mark, cut, position, and stitch larger center circle **5**.
5. Mark, cut, position, and stitch smaller center circle **6**.

Trim block to 12½″ (31.5cm) square.

Block D—Peony Flower Ring

1. Cut 26″ (66cm) of 1″ (2.5cm) bias for ring and stems. Position and stitch four leaf stems. Position and stitch ring.
2. Mark, cut, and position four flower petal pieces, stitching upper edges only and covering end of ring.
3. Mark, cut, and position four flower centers, stitching upper edges only.
4. Mark, cut, position, and stitch four flower bases, covering *lower* edges of flower and end of ring.
5. Mark, cut, position, and stitch four heart-shaped leaves.
6. Mark, cut, position, and stitch four additional leaves.

Trim block to 12½″ (31.5cm) square.

Setting

1. Cut two sashing pieces 3½″ × 12½″ (9cm × 31.5cm). Stitch vertically between blocks **A** and **B**, **C** and **D**.
2. Cut one sashing piece 3½″ × 27½″ (9cm × 69cm). Stitch horizontally between the joined blocks.
3. Cut two side border pieces 4½″ × 27½″ (11.5cm × 69cm). Join the assembled blocks to the borders.
4. Cut two remaining border pieces 4½″ × 35½″ (11.5cm × 89cm). Join to the assembled blocks.

Backing, Quilting, and Binding

Make the backing 39″ (99cm) square.

Quilt by hand or machine. Consider echo quilting or stippling around the block designs. A quilted vine in the borders would be appropriate.

Make 4⅛ yards (4m) of binding for your *Folk Flora* quilt.

Chapter 6

Setting the Quilt

When the individual blocks for your quilt are completed, you are ready to arrange, or *set*, them to make the quilt top. First, carefully measure the blocks to be certain they all finish to the same size. Remember that the unfinished block should measure ½″ (1.5cm) larger than the planned finished size. If you are expecting 12½″ (31.5cm) unfinished blocks, and yours are finishing consistently at 12¼″, 12¾″, or even 12″ (31cm, 32cm, or even 30cm) on all sides, it's not a big deal. You will simply need to adjust sashing and border sizes, and understand that the finished size of the quilt will reflect these adjustments.

We are humans, not machines, and it is not realistic to expect that every block we make, particularly as beginning quiltmakers, will be perfect. However, to improve accuracy, keep these thoughts in mind.

- ◆ Fabric is flexible. It stretches. That can be useful or annoying. Try to make this fact work *for* you, rather than *against* you.
- ◆ No matter how careful we are, there is bound to be at least one piece that wasn't cut exactly the same as the others. Or you may find that one edge of a block has mysteriously grown longer.

If you have assorted humps or an occasional pucker in the finished top, a judicious treatment with the steam iron may be helpful (wish that would work on a few personal humps . . .). It is also possible that the quilting process can disguise a bump here and there. But we are talking *small* anomalies here, folks, not erupting volcanoes! When one block finishes at 12½″ (31.5cm) and the next block measures 12¾″ (32cm), we can probably make it work. However, when that second block measures 13″ (33cm) or more, we're looking at an opportunity to do some repiecing. Pleating the edge of the larger block just isn't a good solution! Easing is fine; gathering is better saved for ruffles.

BLOCKS AND SASHING

There are numerous options for setting your quilt blocks. The most frequently used settings are:

1. Block to block square
2. Block to block, on point, using setting triangles

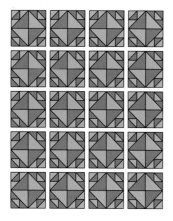

Figure 6.1

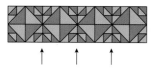

Figure 6.2

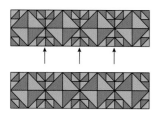

Figure 6.3

Figure 6.4

3. Blocks set square, separated by sashing
4. Blocks set on point, separated by sashing and using setting triangles
5. Blocks set on point, alternating with plain squares and using setting triangles

Other sets can be made by one shape joined repeatedly to itself, with setting pieces formed from that shape. (See *Tumbling Blocks*, page 61; *Texas Star*, page 64, *Inner City* and *Thousand Pyramids*, page 65.)

As a general rule, when sewing the quilt top together, progress from shortest to longest seams, horizontally and vertically, or diagonally.

Block to Block Square (*Birds in the Air*, page 31)

1. Carefully pin the blocks together in rows (fig. 6.1), matching any seam intersections. Remember to butt the matched seams when possible. Stitch (fig. 6.2).
2. Join the rows, matching seams (fig. 6.3).
3. Gently press the joined blocks.

Block to Block, On Point, Using Setting Triangles (*Grandma's Star*, page 43)

This quilt is stitched together in rows on the diagonal (fig. 6.4). To figure the size of the setting triangles (those along the side and at the corners of the quilt top), you must measure your blocks and determine their finished size (unfinished size, minus seam allowance). Some quilters prefer to cut these setting triangles slightly larger than the exact measurements, and trim the edges of the top to size after assembling all the pieces. This allows them to trim the edges square and straight at that time.

Side Triangles

Make the side triangles by using one of the following three methods. A 12″ (30cm) finished block is used as the example.

Method 1. Add ⅞″ (2.5cm) to the finished length of the block side.

$$12'' + \frac{7}{8}'' = 12\frac{7}{8}''$$
$$30cm + 2.5cm = 32.5cm$$

Cut a 12⅞″ (32.5cm) square of fabric; recut the square in half on the diagonal, yielding two side-setting triangles. This places bias edges along the perimeter of the quilt. Handle with care.

Method 2. Figure the diagonal measurement of the finished block (one side of block × 1.414), round off, and add 1¼″ (3.5cm).

$$12'' \times 1.414 = 16.968 \text{ (round up to 17)}; 17'' + 1\frac{1}{4}'' = 18\frac{1}{4}''$$
$$30cm \times 1.414 = 42.4 \text{ (round to 43)}; 43cm + 3.5cm = 46.5cm$$

Cut an 18¼″ (46.5cm) square of fabric; recut the square *twice* on the diagonal, yielding four side-setting triangles with the straight grain or cross-grain on the outside edge.

Here are four additional common block sizes, and the sizes of squares to cut for making side-setting triangles using this second method:

10″ block: 15½″ square (25cm block: 39.5cm square)
9″ block: 14″ square (23cm block: 36.5cm square)
8″ block: 12½″ square (30cm block: 32.5cm square)
6″ block: 9″ square (15cm block: 25.5cm square)

Method 3. Draw the two sides (legs) of a right triangle, based on the finished length of the block side, on a large sheet of graph paper. Carefully follow the intersecting graph paper lines at a 45° angle from the ends of the legs to draw the long side (hypotenuse) of the triangle. Make your template from this drawing (fig. 6.5).

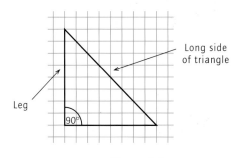

Figure 6.5

Personally, I don't mind dealing with bias edges, and I am more confident cutting smaller squares. Should you prefer not to have that long bias edge, or you are working with fabric that would look best cut one triangle at a time, you now have the know-how to handle each situation.

Corner Triangles

Corner triangles can also be made in one of three ways. Again, a 12″ (30cm) block is used as the example.

Method 1. Add 1¼″ (3.5cm) to the finished length of one side of the block.

$$12″ + 1¼″ = 13¼″$$
$$30cm + 3.5cm = 33.5cm$$

Cut a 13¼″ (33.5cm) square. Recut the square *twice* on the diagonal, yielding four corner triangles (again putting bias edges on the outside of the quilt).

Method 2. Figure the diagonal measurement of the block.

$$12″ \times 1.414 = 16.968$$
$$30cm \times 1.414 = 42.4cm–round\ to\ 43cm$$

Round up to 17″ (43cm). Divide in half.

$$17″ \div 2 = 8½″$$
$$43cm / 2 = 21.5cm$$

Add ⅞″ (2.5cm).

$$8½″ + ⅞″ = 9⅜″$$
$$21.5cm + 2.5cm = 24cm$$

Cut a 9⅜″ (24cm) square. Recut the square *once* on the diagonal. Two squares yield four corner triangles.

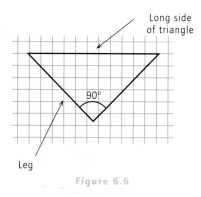

Figure 6.6

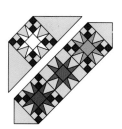

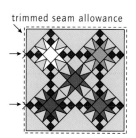

Figure 6.7

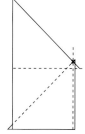

Figure 6.8

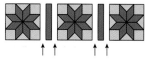

Figure 6.9

Method 3. Draw a right triangle measuring 12" (30cm) on its long side (hypotenuse) on a sheet of graph paper. Carefully follow the intersecting graph paper lines, at a 45° angle from the ends of the 12" (30cm) line, to draw the sides (legs) of the triangle. Be certain that these two sides are equal in length, and that they come together in a 90° angle, or square corner. Make your template from this drawing (fig. 6.6).

Additional rotary rulers, such as a 12" or 16" (30cm or 40cm) square and several triangle rulers can make this task easier. See Appendix 2 for additional information.

Quilt Top Layout

Once you have the side and corner setting triangles prepared, lay out the blocks and triangles so that you can clearly see how they will go together.

1. Pin the diagonal rows, matching seams. Stitch (fig. 6.7).
2. Pin and stitch the diagonal rows together, matching seams and remembering that the triangle points will overlap at the outside edges (fig. 6.8).
3. Add the two remaining corner triangles.
4. Press the top, taking care not to stretch the edges. If any edge of the quilt top looks slightly wobbly and can be trimmed without compromising the ¼" (0.75cm) seam allowance, do so now. This can be done using the long rotary ruler. Place the ¼" (0.75cm) mark of the ruler's long side at the X where the diagonal seams cross, hold firmly, and trim carefully (fig. 6.9). This is *not* a good time to let the ruler slip!

Blocks Set Square, Separated by Sashing (*Ohio Star*, page 37; *LeMoyne Star*, page 55)

1. Always begin by measuring your blocks. To help with consistency of size and making a flat quilt top, cut all sashing pieces for similar placement the same size. Ease any blocks that are slightly longer on a side; gently encourage growth of any slightly shorter sides (yes, this is one instance where I encourage you to stretch fabric).
2. Measure and cut the vertical sashing. For hand piecing, cut the sashing pieces, including seam allowances, *then* mark the seamlines, taking care not to stretch the edges.
3. Pin and stitch the short vertical sashes into the horizontal rows (fig. 6.10). Keep the blocks on top as you stitch, allowing you to see any seam intersections.
4. Measure and cut the horizontal sashing strips.
5. Pin and stitch the horizontal sashing strips between the rows of blocks, again keeping blocks on top. To keep the blocks aligned above and below the sashing, it is helpful to measure and mark the seam placement on both long edges of the sashing strip (fig. 6.11) or to create a sashing with cornerstones (fig. 6.12). The *LeMoyne Star* quilt shows this type of sashing.

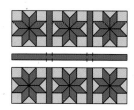

Figure 6.11

6. Measure and cut the side sashing (which may also be called an inner border). Pin and stitch, keeping the blocks on top (fig. 6.13).

7. Measure and cut the top and bottom sashing (inner border, as in Step 6). Pin and stitch (fig 6.14).

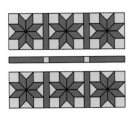

Figure 6.12

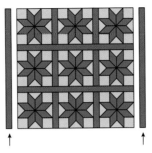

Figure 6.13

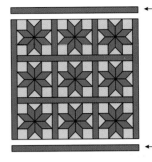

Figure 6.14

Blocks Set On Point, Separated by Sashing, Using Setting Triangles (*Hot Tropic Hearts*, page 131)

This method is a combination of the second and third methods.

1. Measure and cut the short sashing strips.

2. Pin and stitch the strips and blocks to make the diagonal rows (fig. 6.15).

3. Measure and cut the long sashing strips, *slightly longer* than needed. Measure and mark seam placement from the center to the ends on both long sides of the strip (fig. 6.16), or use cornerstones (as in Step 5 above), making the section extra long on each end.

4. Pin and stitch the diagonal rows together. Trim off the excess at the end of the long sashing strips in line with the setting triangles. Watch the seam allowance—don't trim too much!

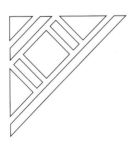

Figure 6.15

Figure 6.16

Blocks Set On Point, Alternating with Plain Squares, Using Setting Triangles (*Nine-Patch*, page 25)

This method is the same as Block to Block, On Point, Using Setting Triangles (page 91); it just has a different look (fig 6.17). As you lay out the blocks and tri-angles, the plain blocks will alternate with your design blocks in the diagonal rows. This set allows you to sew blocks together matching edges and corners of the blocks, not interior seams. It also opens up more space for decorative quilting.

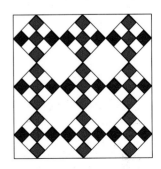

Figure 6.17

BORDERS

Many quilts are completed by some kind of border treatment. For a wall quilt, the border often resembles a picture frame. Bed quilts can be made with large borders surrounding the central (mattress top) design to cover the sides of the bed. Some quilts do not have borders at all. This depends ultimately on the quiltmaker's preference.

Should you desire a border for your quilt, there are three basic types from which to choose: *plain, pieced,* and *appliquéd.* As you become more confident with your stitching and designing, you may wish to combine types.

The most important steps to a successful border are *accurate measuring* and *controlling the fabric grain.*

- ◆ Remember to measure the sides of the quilt top at least 6" (15cm) inside any edge, and to *use half of the difference* in the measurements of opposite sides to determine the base border length measurement (fig. 6.18). The key here is a reasonable difference; anything exceeding 1¼" (3.5cm) creates real problems and must be dealt with before adding borders.
- ◆ Once the measurements are accurate, the grain of the fabric should not cause too much concern. Just remember that pieces cut on the crosswise grain will stretch more than straight grain (lengthwise) pieces. Pin and stitch accordingly.

If the fabric choice for the border is a solid or a nondirectional print (the clowns are upside-down and sideways, as well as upright), you may elect to cut the borders across the fabric from selvage to selvage (cross-grain). This is the most economical use of the yardage, but remember that it can stretch when stitched in place by machine. If the border fabric has a directional print (all of the bears are riding their unicycles in an upright position, parallel to the selvage), whether to cut crosswise or lengthwise depends on how the design is printed and how you wish it to be oriented in the border.

If you must sew pieces of one fabric together to make sufficient length for a border, try to match any design motifs. If using solid fabric, the seam will be less noticeable if cut and stitched at a 45° angle. Another option is to give the quilt a folk art look by piecing several different fabrics into one border.

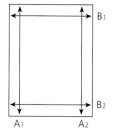

Side A₁ = 45½" (116cm)   Side B₁ = 35" (89cm)
Side A₂ = 44½" (114cm)   Side B₂ = 34½" (88cm)
Base border measurement A = 45" (115cm)   Base border measurement B = 34¾" (88.2cm)

Figure 6.18

Plain Borders

These borders are created with lengths of fabric surrounding a pieced or appliquéd center. There may be one, two, or three borders; there really is no "proper" amount. Balance the size of the border(s) with the size of the blocks, both for ease of construction and visual harmony. A good way to determine size is to use a number that is contained within multiples of the block size. An example, for a 12″ block:

$$2 \times 6 = 12; 3 \times 4 = 12$$
Possible border sizes: 6″, 4″, 3″, 2″

An example, for a 30cm block:

$$5 \times 6 = 30; 10 \times 3 = 30$$
Possible border sizes: 10cm, 6cm, 5cm, 3cm

The 2″ and 3″ choices would work well as sashing sizes or inner borders. You might also choose to feature a fabulous fabric or special large quilting design on a 12″ or 15″ border. Solid fabrics will show off lots of quilting in these areas. Patterned fabrics focus attention on their designs and, while they still need to be adequately quilted, the quilting will not be as visible. For your first efforts, you might consider this a blessing, not a liability!

Straight-Seam Corners

Making a plain border with straight-seam corners is probably the easiest for most quilters (fig. 6.19).

1. Measure the sides of the quilt top (see fig. 6.18). Cut the side border pieces and pin them to the assembled blocks, right sides together, using the quartering method. Fold the border pieces in half lengthwise *twice*, putting a pin at the halfway mark and the two quarter marks (fig. 6.20). Do the same with the sides of the quilt top. Match these, pinning the blocks on top of the border piece. This arrangement has advantages for both hand and machine sewing.

   ◆ Hand: Keeping the blocks on top allows you to easily see the marked seamlines and stitch point to point.
   ◆ Machine: You can see the seams of a pieced center and monitor them as they pass under the presser foot so they don't flip or bunch.
   ◆ Machine: If the border piece has been cut crosswise, keeping it against the feed dogs helps reduce stretching.

   Stitch the side border seams.
2. Measure across the top and bottom of the quilt, including the width of the side borders. Determine the proper length for these border pieces (B). Cut and pin them, right sides together, as above. Stitch.

If you wish to use this method for more than one border, each must be added incrementally (much like a *Courthouse Square* block is made). Measure carefully and don't allow the outside edges to stretch or "grow."

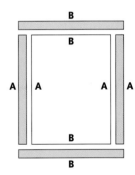

Figure 6.19

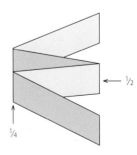

Figure 6.20

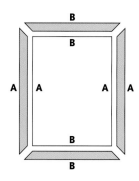

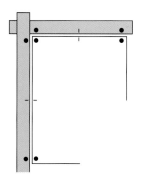

Figure 6.21

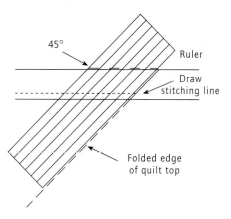

Figure 6.22

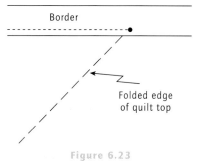

Figure 6.23

Figure 6.24

Mitered Corners

Often a quilt border looks best with mitered corners (fig. 6.21). These are sewn at a 45° angle to the edge of the border. They are well suited to showcasing fabrics such as stripes and large border prints, as well as to finishing quilt patterns containing lots of right triangles.

1. Measure the two sets of opposite sides on the quilt top. Determine the **A** length and **B** length (halving the differences if necessary). For this procedure, the border pieces are cut longer than the actual measurements and trimmed after the miters are sewn. Therefore, the total length of each **A** border will be:

   measurement **A** + width of border **B** (× 2) + 3″ (37.5cm)

   Example: 40½″ + 6½″ (× 2) + 3″ = 56½″
                      (40½″ + 13″ + 3″ = 56½″)
            103cm + 16.5cm (× 2) + 7.5cm = 143.5cm
               (103cm + 33cm + 7.5cm = 143.5cm)

   The total length of each **B** border will be:

   measurement **B** + width of border **A** (× 2) + 3″ (7.5cm)

   Example: 30½″ + 6½″ (× 2) + 3″ = 46½″
                      (30½″ + 13″ + 3″ = 46½″)
            78cm + 16.5cm (× 2) + 7.5cm = 118.5cm
                (78cm + 33cm + 7.5cm = 118.5cm)

   On the quilt top, mark the center of each side and the ¼″ (0.75cm) at each corner. Mark the center of each border piece. From these centers, measure out half the distance of the matching sides and mark at each end (fig. 6.22). For example, if side **A** = 40½″ (103cm), measure 20″ (51cm) from the center of border piece **A** toward each end and mark this point. This matches the ¼″ (0.75cm) mark at each end of the side.

2. Pin each border to its corresponding side, matching centers and end points. Stitch, either by hand or machine, from end point to end point. Secure the seam with several backstitches at each end. After all four border pieces are attached, make the miters.

3. At one corner, fold the quilt top diagonally, right sides together, aligning the edges of the two adjoining border pieces. Push the two seam allowances toward the quilt top. Pin the borders together, carefully matching the seams (fig. 6.23). Place the 45° ruler line at the outside edge of the border so that the edge of the ruler passes through the end point of the stitched seam, matching the folded edge of the quilt top (fig. 6.24). Draw a line along this ruler edge. Stitch on this line, using several backstitches where it meets the seam end point. After checking that the corner is flat, trim the seam to ½″ (1.5cm) and press open. Repeat until all four corners are mitered. Then press the quilt top seam toward the border.

This method works well for multiple borders. First sew the border lengths for each side together; then treat them as one fabric. When mitering the corners, pin carefully at each seam to keep the fabrics properly aligned. (You can again use the technique of turning one seam to the left and one to the right.) For striped fabric, cut each border identically in relation to the stripes. At the corners, carefully match and pin the stripes to prevent them from shifting when stitching the seam at a 45° angle.

Pieced Borders

A pieced border can beautifully complete the overall design of a quilt. Usually it will carry one or more shapes from the central portion into the edges of the quilt. However, a pieced border can be equally effective on an appliqué quilt, such as a simple sawtooth border surrounding wonderful Baltimore Album blocks.

To determine the shapes to be used in the border and their placement, the easiest method is to draw out the size and set of the blocks on graph paper. Using eight-squares-to-the-inch paper allows enough room to plan at least two full sides. Those who have computer skills may have a graphics program useful for drawing a design.

The major challenge with borders of this type is working out how to turn the corners. Using sizes that appear in the blocks themselves often helps to make this easier. Three different pieced borders drawn to scale are shown as examples for the quilts *Birds in the Air* (fig. 6.25), *Grandma's Star* (fig. 6.26), or *Folk Flora* (fig. 6.27).

Remember to figure the sizes carefully, adding ¼" (0.75cm) seam allowances. Also try testing a corner by making it from practice fabric. Check the Bibliography for an excellent source of information and ideas for borders.

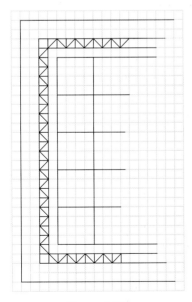

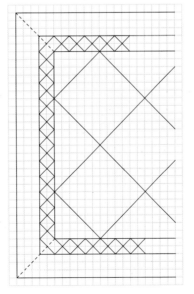

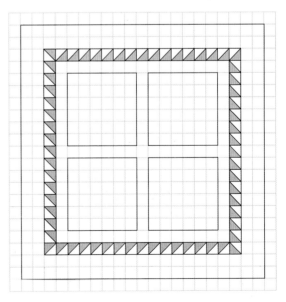

Figure 6.25   Figure 6.26   Figure 6.27

Appliquéd Borders

Appliqué provides a glorious, free-spirited way to use fabric. Just as in appliqué blocks, you can create your own real or fantasy worlds in appliquéd borders. Use them to finish telling the story of the quilt blocks; literally twine (vine) around the floral blocks; wrap up a central theme with swags, banners, or ribbons; or add a soft touch to piecework. The appliqué is done on a plain border base.

To plan most easily, begin with the corners. All four need not be identical. You have lots of freedom with appliqué. Next, devise the centers of the sides if you wish to feature something there. Then decide how to join these two areas together. Or plan to divide the side border and end border into evenly spaced swags or ribbons. Graph paper can be helpful, as well as using the "paper doll" approach. Inexpensive adding-machine tape works really well. Cut a length of tape to equal a length of border. By carefully folding it in half, then in half again, and so on, you can easily reach a workable size for your swag. Unfold the tape and it will show you immediately how many units are needed for that border.

Use strips of inexpensive paper that measure the same as the border width to sketch each part of the border. If a design is repeated, you need only draw it once on a corresponding length of paper. Transfer the motifs and their placement onto the fabric border strips. Make templates in whichever style you prefer.

It is easier to appliqué most of the border length *before* attaching it to the quilt. Wait to finish the corner appliqué until after each border is stitched in place. Then complete the work that crosses over the corner seams.

Relax and enjoy the wonderful creative possibilities for all kinds of appliquéd borders. Consider carrying parts of the border appliqué over into the blocks or out onto an additional plain border. Experiment with your ideas, making this part of your quilt truly unique.

Chapter 7

Preparing to Quilt

Once the quilt top is completed, it is time to begin the quilting process. In this chapter, you will learn how to make the "quilt sandwich," combining the quilt top with backing and batting, ready for basting. You will also find help in selecting a quilting design for your quilt and marking it onto the quilt top.

PREPARING THE QUILT TOP

To make sure your quilt top is ready, look it over carefully and check all piecework and appliqué for loose or open seams; repair if necessary. Carefully trim sewing threads or raveling fabric threads. Make the back neat and tidy, because loose threads have a sneaky tendency to settle under lighter fabrics, giving the impression of worms crawling under your quilt top! It detracts from all the beauty you've created.

Figure 7.1

If light and dark fabrics are seamed together and cannot be pressed toward the darker fabric, grade back the darker seam allowance so that it stays *behind* the lighter seam allowance (fig. 7.1). Trim carefully! This prevents "shadowing," the impression of a darker line along the seam allowance.

Were you indulging in something that left telltale fingerprints or spots on your quilt top? Remove any spots or stains now, before pressing or quilting. The last step is to give the top a final pressing and set it aside to await basting. To keep the top from wrinkling, gently fold it in half, thirds, or fourths across the smallest width. Then suspend from a skirt hanger with clips. The result, viewed from the side, looks like a teardrop (fig. 7.2).

Figure 7.2

MAKING THE BACKING

The backing for a quilt may be made in a variety of ways. If it is a small quilt, less than 40″ (100cm) wide, almost all fabrics suitable for quilts will also work as backing fabrics. For quilts wider than 40″ (100cm), other options need to be considered. A limited selection of 90″-wide (230cm-wide) and 108″-wide (275cm-wide) fabrics is available. Or you can seam lengths of fabric together. Choose the most efficient and economical use of the fabric, as long as the result is pleasing for you and the quilt.

I enjoy and encourage making interesting backs for quilts. Piece together large leftovers from the top or find other fabrics that complement your original choices. You may even want to stitch a few more blocks of the top design and piece them into the backing fabric.

If you plan to hand quilt, avoid tightly woven fabrics such as pima cotton or percale sheeting for backing. Keep in mind that busily patterned fabric will make the quilting stitches on the back less visible. This may be a good choice until you're ready to proudly show off that part of your handiwork.

Measuring and Stitching the Quilt Backing

1. Prepare the backing fabric as you did the top.
2. Make the backing *at least 2" (5cm) larger* on all sides than the quilt top. If the quilt top measures 40" × 55" (100cm × 140cm), the backing should measure *at least* 44" × 59" (112cm × 150cm). Should you wish to have a bit more backing to roll over the edges of the batting (to keep it from tearing or shedding as you quilt), add 3" to 4" (7cm to 9cm) all around.
3. Avoid placing a seam down the middle of the back when joining two long lengths of fabric. To sew together two pieces of 44"-wide (112cm-wide) fabric, pin the two lengths, right sides together, on both selvage edges. Sew both sides, using ¾" (2cm) seams (larger if the selvage edges are wider than ½" (1.5cm). Cut *one* of the lengths in half, lengthwise, between the two seams. Trim off all selvage edges. The result is two seams closer to each side of the back, rather than one seam down the middle.
4. Press the back, pressing the seams to one side.

SELECTING THE BATTING

Your choice of quilting technique will influence the batting selection. I find cotton/polyester blend batts to be excellent choices for machine quilting because the layers tend to shift less. However, 100% polyester batts are easier to hand quilt, especially for beginners.

Loft (height) and *density* (thickness) of the batting are also considerations. Batting with low loft is suitable for both hand and machine quilting and results in an older, flatter look. Traditional, or regular, loft is slightly more challenging to quilt by hand and results in greater definition of the sculpted look produced by the quilting stitches. Higher lofts (such as extra, ultra, or "fat") are intended for hand tying, as in comforters, and are not suitable for either hand or machine quilting. A dense batting is not a problem for machine quilting; it can make hand quilting more difficult.

Test as many battings as you can. Make a small sample, using the type of thread and style of quilting you have chosen for a particular project. You'll know quickly which of the test batts will produce the result you want.

Specialty battings, such as wool and silk, are also available. Wool is expensive, but makes a wonderfully warm quilt and is quite pleasant to hand quilt. Follow the manufacturer's instructions for handling. Silk batting is more suitable for garments because of its thinness and soft drape.

Check to see if your batting selection has any manufacturer's instructions for preparation before quilting. In general, allow the batting some time to "breathe" before basting: take it out of the package and either spread it out on a bed overnight or put it in the dryer and fluff it for 8 to 10 minutes on a *non-heat* setting. If you use a cotton batting, you may wish to soak and preshrink it. This will make hand quilting easier. It also keeps the batt flatter when the quilt is washed. Follow the manufacturer's instructions *carefully*. *Never* agitate a batt in the washing machine.

BASTING THE QUILT SANDWICH

Most of us quilt either by hand, using a hoop or a small frame, or by machine, using our regular home sewing machines. In order to do that, the three layers—backing, batting, and top—must be held together. Remember that a good basting job will facilitate a good quilting experience.

Assembling the Layers

1. Spread out the backing layer, *wrong side up*, on the most comfortable-to-reach hard surface that you can find. A large table or group of tables is ideal.
2. Gently stretch the backing taut, so that it is nice and flat, fastening it to the basting surface. This can be done with 1″ (2.5cm) masking (not duct!) tape or large office binder clips. If you have someone to work across the table from you, smooth, straighten, and fasten the long sides first, from the middle to the corners. Stay directly opposite each other as you work (fig. 7.3). If you are working alone, fasten one side completely; then move to the opposite side and fasten that. Repeat for the remaining two sides.
3. Center the batting on top of the backing. Smooth it out, taking care not to snag or rip it. Check for any thin or thick spots, gently redistributing the surrounding fibers with your fingertips.
4. Place the completed quilt top, centered and right side up, on the batting. Smooth it gently. Stand at one end and look down the length of the quilt to see if the seams and borders are straight. Use your fingertips to reposition wobbly seams, or try lifting one end of the quilt top slightly away from the batting and shifting it to the left or right. When it's as square as possible, your quilt sandwich is ready for basting.

    If the size of your work surface permits you to baste only a section of the quilt at a time, begin in the center. Thoroughly baste the center area, then reposition as many times as necessary to reach the edges. Be certain that you have centered everything, so there are no unfortunate surprises when you reach an outside edge. Fold each layer in half with a marked center point before you set it on the basting surface to make this process easier.

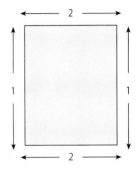

Figure 7.3

Begin basting the three layers together, using one of the following methods. Some quilters thread baste for both hand and machine quilting; others prefer to pin baste for machine—or both. My experience is that thread basting is the best choice for hand quilting and pin basting is more satisfactory for machine quilting.

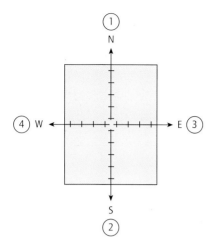

Figure 7.4

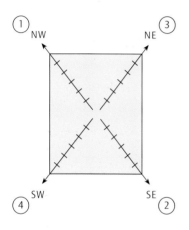

Figure 7.5

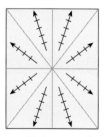

Figure 7.6

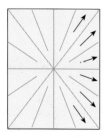

Figure 7.7

Thread Basting

To anchor the layers, first pin through all thicknesses with large, heavy straight pins. Remember that you are pinning through all three layers. Begin in the center, always moving toward an outside edge, gently smoothing the quilt top as you go. Think of compass points and pin first in the **N**, **S**, **E**, and **W** directions. Note that the pins are placed *parallel* to the edge you are moving toward (fig. 7.4). For any project over 30" (75cm) square, placing the pins 4" to 6" (10cm to 15cm) apart is fine. For smaller projects, use 3" to 4" (7cm to 10cm) intervals. Next, pin from the center to each of the four corners (**NW**, **NE**, **SE**, **SW**), placing the pins as indicated (fig. 7.5).

For a small piece, this should be enough rows of pins to hold the layers adequately. For anything 30" (75cm) square or larger, add another row of pins between each existing row. Note that you can begin pinning 8" to 10" (20cm to 25cm) away from the center (fig 7.6). When this is done, if there are still unpinned areas 12" (30cm) or larger, either continue with radiating rows until these are secure (fig. 7.7), or just place a few more pins at 6" (15cm) intervals to complete the section.

To thread baste the quilt, use white basting thread (available reasonably priced). Using white thread, as opposed to any leftover colors or antique thread from Aunt Somebody's sewing box, eliminates the possibility of leaving permanent dots of unwanted color on your quilt top. Trust me, it has happened! Use a long needle (or you may prefer a curved one) for basting. I like size 7 John James Long Darners or EZ Gold Eye Quilt Basting needles (size 7). Small, thin needles just don't stand up well to the rigors of basting.

Baste along the lines where you have pinned, pulling the pins out as you go. If the quilting pattern is already marked on the quilt top, avoid basting stitches directly on marked lines if possible. Thread the needle and lay the spool of thread in the center of the quilt. Don't cut any thread yet. Stitch from the center to **N** on our imaginary compass, making the stitch on top approximately 1½" (4cm) long and the stitch on the back approximately ¾" (2cm) long (fig. 7.8). The thread will keep unwinding off the spool as you sew. Take several backstitches at the edge and unthread the needle.

Return to the center of the quilt. Take the spool and gently pull on the thread to tighten the basting stitches (you should see the batting compress under them). Now wind off enough thread to complete stitching to **S** by extending the thread at least 4" (10cm) for a small project and 8" to 10" (20 cm to 25cm) for larger quilts. Cut it, thread the needle, and stitch to S (fig. 7.9). Tighten the stitches, and finish with several backstitches.

If you are basting more than 30" (75cm), it makes sense to tighten the stitches several times before you reach the edge. Also, you do not have to pull the thread completely through with each stitch. If you have any difficulty making basting stitches through all the layers, consider using a spoon to help (not your best silver!). Hold the spoon upright with the bowl facing your needle. Pushing down on the spoon handle compresses the batting, and as the needle moves forward, it rides right up into the bowl of the spoon. This makes it easier to grasp the needle and pull it through.

Baste the **E–W** and corner-to-corner pinning lines in the same fashion as **N–S**. This eliminates a cluster of knots in the center of the quilt. Remember to remove the pins from each line as you thread baste.

When the longest pin lines are secured, move around the quilt (in a counterclockwise direction for right-handers, clockwise for left-handers, keeping you stitching from center to edge in the most natural fashion) and baste the shorter pin lines.

The last basting to be done is parallel to all the edges of the quilt, stitching approximately ¾″ (2cm) from each edge (fig. 7.10). You can knot at each end of this thread. Remove the tape, releasing the backing. At this time, you may also wish to fold the edge of the backing around to the front and baste it down over the raw edge of the batting. Now you can celebrate!

Pin Basting

Machine quilting seems best served by the use of small nickel-plated (avoids rusting) safety pins to hold the quilt layers together. These pins should be size 1 or size 0 with sharp points. Larger pins make too large a hole in the fabrics.

Prepare the layers in the same way as for thread basting. When ready to pin, follow the same compass placement—with several important exceptions:

- ◆ Do not place the pins directly along a line where you know you will stitch, such as in-the-ditch along a seam, or diagonally through a star pattern. Shift the pins to the left or right.
- ◆ If you have marked a quilting motif in an open block, place the pins around and in the center of the design. Leave enough room for the darning foot to move between the pins.

It is impossible to place all the pins needed to adequately hold the layers so that they don't interfere with a stitching line from time to time. While working at the machine, simply remove the pins as you go along.

Insert all the safety pins while the backing is secured, but *wait to close them until after the backing is released*. There are also several products on the market that facilitate closing the pins (see Appendix 2).

To properly baste the quilt takes a good quantity of pins. Don't shortchange this step. A crib to twin size will require 200 or more pins. Adequate pinning reduces shifting of the layers, and bunching or tucking on the back.

SELECTING THE QUILTING DESIGN

The choice of quilting design should enhance the piecework or appliqué. After all, it really isn't a quilt until it's quilted! The following are the most commonly used quilting styles.

- ◆ In-the-ditch: to stitch closely along a seamline on the opposite side from where the seams have been pressed. This is the least visible location for quilting stitches (fig. 7.11)
- ◆ At the quarter inch (0.75cm): to stitch ¼″ (0.75cm) inside the seamlines of each patchwork shape (fig. 7.12)

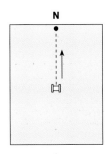

Figure 7.8

Figure 7.9

Figure 7.10

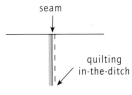

Figure 7.11

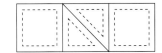

Figure 7.12

Figure 7.13

Figure 7.14

Figure 7.15

Use pencils and washout markers before basting; chalk pencils, pressure markers, and ¼" (0.75cm) masking tape as you quilt. A combination of methods may be the best solution. Regardless of which tool(s) you select, always mark lightly and remove any marks as quickly as possible.

- In a grid: to stitch an area, such as the background of a block, in parallel, diagonally crossing lines (fig. 7.13)
- Echo: to stitch a quilting line at ¼" (0.75cm) around the outside of a shape, such as a flower; this is usually repeated many times (fig. 7.14)
- Stipple or meander: to stitch a continuous line that resembles lots of jigsaw puzzle pieces; it gives texture to background areas and may be spread out or dense; these lines do not cross each other as grid lines do (fig. 7.15)
- Outline: (a) to stitch close to the outside edge of a shape (sort of in-the-ditch for appliqué); (b) to stitch on the design lines of patterned fabric; (c) to stitch along a marked linear design, such as a cable or the shape of an object

An important consideration in choosing a quilting design is whether all the stitching will be visible or blend into patterned fabric. Make the decision based on what will serve both you and the quilt.

Marking the Quilt Top

Some types of quilting do not need to be marked on the quilt top before you begin to stitch: in-the-ditch, echo, outline (a) and (b), and meander. Stitching the first three types requires following something that already exists, such as a seamline or an appliqué shape. The meander stitch fills an open space by freely twisting and turning. Grids and linear shapes, however, need to be marked on the quilt top. Marking tools are available in a variety of forms.

- Pencils—Many colors and styles are available. Use only those that will rinse out. Always test on scrap fabrics before marking. There are pencils that can make a very fine line, and those that can be seen on dark fabrics.
- Chalk pencils—The marks from these pencils will wash out. However, since they can also rub off as you work, use them on a small section at a time. They make a relatively fat line. Their marks can be seen on dark fabrics. Do not substitute tailor's chalk.
- Washout markers—They make a bright blue or purple line. The marks are created with chemicals that can leave stains unless completely *rinsed* out of both fabric and batting. The color is easy to see on light and medium-value fabrics.
- Pressure markers—A pointer and creaser tool or Hera marker make a crease in the quilt surface. You then stitch along the crease. There is no visible mark, so it can be difficult to see. However, this may also be an advantage, as there is no residue. They are good for straight-line work.
- ¼" (0.75cm) masking tape—This is placed along seamlines as a guideline for stitching at the quarter inch (0.75cm). The tape should be totally removed after each stitching session. It may mark the fabric if left on too long.

Chapter 8

Hand Quilting

Although many new and experienced quiltmakers prefer to make their quilt tops by machine, they often find that quilting by hand is well worth the time and effort it takes. Once you master the quilting stitch and develop a rhythm, hand quilting can be a relaxing and enjoyable pastime.

HOOPS AND FRAMES

It is possible to quilt by hand in a hoop or frame, or without either one. Quilting by hand can also be done with the quilt mounted in a floor frame. Not everyone has the space or inclination for that, although many of us have spent wonderful shared hours around a frame, stitching on a guild or group quilt.

Working with a hoop provides stability for the stitching, though it can be awkward at first. You are about to use a needle in an unfamiliar way. Stick with it—you can do it! It is a good idea to assemble a practice piece. Make a large *Nine-Patch* by stitching together nine 6½" (16cm) squares. Cut a 20" (50cm) square of both backing and batting. Baste these three layers together. Use this piece to practice stitching in-the-ditch, at the quarter inch, gridwork, or linear shapes such as hearts, leaves, or flowers in the open squares. Test needle sizes and types of thread on this practice piece (fig. 8.1).

When you are ready to begin quilting the "real" quilt, stitch the center area first. Then move toward the outer edges.

Hoops have two parts, an inner ring and an outer ring, which can be loosened or tightened. Release the fastener on the outer ring, position the inner ring under the quilt section where you will begin stitching, and gently push down the outer ring over both. Once the outer ring is in place, tighten the fastening screw. The quilt should be smooth, flat, and taut, but not pulled out of shape.

Pipe frames have a square or rectangular pipe unit and four long, open pipe pieces that snap over the frame, holding the quilt in place. Center the pipe unit under the quilt section where you will begin stitching and carefully snap on the clamp pieces, one at a time. Work in opposite pairs. These clamp pieces can be rotated slightly around the pipe frame to tighten or loosen the tautness of the quilt. Smooth out any pleats or wrinkles above or below the frame before beginning to stitch.

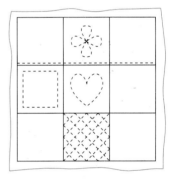

Figure 8.1

Knot

Figure 8.2

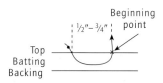

Figure 8.3

Beginning
point

½"–¾"

Top
Batting
Backing

Figure 8.4

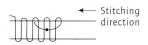

Figure 8.5

← Stitching
    direction

Figure 8.6

Figure 8.7

Figure 8.8

HOW TO BEGIN QUILTING

Thread a no. 9 or no. 10 betweens needle, and cut an 18" (45cm) length of quilting thread (about the distance from the tip of your middle finger to your elbow). Some quilters like to thread a pack of needles onto a spool of thread. Then they cut off a length of thread with one needle attached at a time (fig. 8.2). It's one way to streamline the threading process. Put one small knot at the end of the thread (fig. 8.3).

Plan to stitch in one of two directions: across your body or toward your body. If you are right-handed and stitching a line from right to left, begin stitching in this fashion: insert the needle about ½" (1.5cm) ahead of where you will make the first stitch. Push the needle under the line of stitching, through the batting layer only, and bring it up where you will begin (fig. 8.4). *Reverse this procedure if you are left-handed.*

Pull the thread until the knot pops down through the top. Pull the thread a little more until the knot is about halfway from where it entered the top to where the needle exited the top (fig. 8.5). Now begin to stitch. This effectively anchors the thread by stitching over the end (fig. 8.6).

Making the Quilting Stitch

Put your non-needle hand, palm side up, under the hoop and place your middle finger under the stitching line. This underneath finger will push up on the quilt top (fig. 8.7). Don't try to grasp the hoop with your thumb as you do this. Even though it may seem possible with the small practice piece, you can't hold onto the hoop and half of a quilt. Just don't start the habit.

Put the thimble on the middle finger of your needle hand. Rest your hand on its side, pinkie finger against the quilt. It will naturally assume a curved position (fig. 8.8). Lift up the index finger and move the thimble toward your thumb (fig. 8.9). This is the motion you will make as you do the quilting stitch. It's almost like a crab claw motion—thumb sideways, thimble push, thumb sideways, thimble push . . .

To do the next part of this crab claw motion requires understanding how the underneath finger and the upper thumb work together. The finger pushes up a ridge of quilt, and the thumb pushes down, so that the ridge is between the thumb and the needle (fig. 8.10). This is not a huge tug-of-war. It's more like gentle pressure exerted in opposite directions. The needle is inserted straight up and down (not at an angle) until it touches the underneath finger. Think about this; it's not very far!

A common question at this point is, "Might I puncture my underneath finger?" Yes, you probably will, until you build up a callus—or use any one of a number of finger protectors. If you do get blood on the quilt backing, it can easily be removed with cold water.

As soon as the needle touches the underneath finger, use the thimble (not your index finger) to swing the needle point back toward the quilt surface, through the ridge that the thumb has made. Push the top of the needle toward the quilt surface, and then squeeze it forward toward your thumb (fig. 8.11).

The amount of needle showing here will be the size of your next stitch. Using the thimble, bring the needle upright again (you will be pulling the quilt with you), insert, swing, squeeze, pushing the needle all the way through and out of the quilt. Pull some, not all, of the quilting thread through at this time.

Repeat. *Insert, swing, squeeze, insert, swing, squeeze, pull.* You are loading three stitches onto the needle with each of these repetitions, making a total of four stitches—two on the back and two on the top. Pull all of the quilting thread through after doing this several times. Be certain that the batting is compressing under the stitches.

Figure 8.9

At times you may be able to load more stitches onto the needle. At other times, such as stitching around some curves, you may have to take one stitch at a time.

When learning the quilting stitch, it's not important to get worked up about the number of stitches to the inch (cm). It's far more important to work on making even stitches that are the same size on the top and the back. Avoid "pick" stitches—tiny stitches on the back where the needle has barely caught any threads. Practice the motion of swinging the needle so you get a feel of "scooping up" the back fabric. The more you stitch, the smaller the stitches will become, and the easier it will become to fall into the rhythm of the motion of the needle.

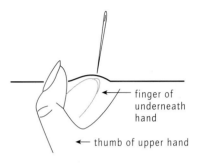

finger of underneath hand

thumb of upper hand

Figure 8.10

A Trick or Two

Use this little trick with the needle to pass the quilting thread from one area to another. Holding the thread to one side with your non-needle hand, insert the needle into the hole from which it just exited, keeping the needle just under the quilt top. Push the needle as far as its length will permit, bringing only the point out on top. Carefully grasp the point, swinging the eye end of the needle around under the quilt top. With your thimble, push the point end of the needle to pop out the eye end at the next quilting line (fig. 8.12). Pull the entire needle and thread out. Begin stitching.

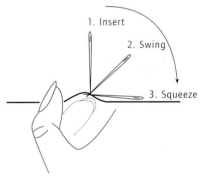

1. Insert

2. Swing

3. Squeeze

Figure 8.11

One more trick—hiding the thread tail. When you begin or end a line of stitching, the thread tail may not disappear with the knot. Insert the needle just under the quilt top near the short bit of leftover thread. Swing the needle so that it will catch the thread and pull the thread tail under the fabric (fig. 8.13). Voilà!

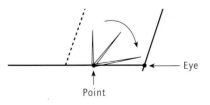

Eye

Point

Figure 8.12

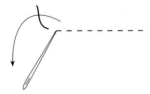

Figure 8.13

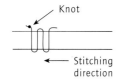

Figure 8.14

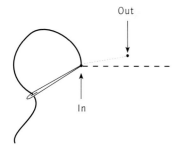

Figure 8.15

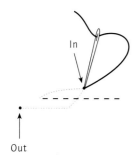

Figure 8.16

Figure 8.17

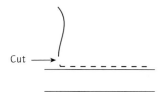

Figure 8.18

Figure 8.19

How to End

To end a thread, put a knot on the thread by looping it and passing the needle through the loop. Don't pull the knot tight until it is right at the surface of the quilt where the thread exits the top (fig. 8.14). With your non-needle hand, gently pull the thread to the side and insert the needle into the hole it just came out of. Keep the point of the needle in the batting layer and let it exit the quilt about ½" (1.5cm) back along the line of stitches, as shown (fig. 8.15). Pop the knot back into the batting layer as you pull out the needle and thread.

You may now choose to put another knot on the thread, again close to the quilt surface. Once more, hold the thread away from its exit point and reinsert the needle into the batting layer. Guide the needle between two stitches and push it back along the stitching line and beyond as far as it will go (fig. 8.16). The thread has made a U-turn around the end of the stitching line (fig. 8.17).

Bring the needle and thread out of the quilt top and *carefully* clip the thread, holding the scissors parallel to the quilt surface (fig. 8.18).

To begin the next thread, start about ½" (1.5cm) ahead of the hole where you buried the end knot of the previous thread. Insert the needle and knotted thread, bringing the needle up through that hole (fig. 8.19). Begin stitching. In this way, there are no missing stitches on the top or back of the quilt. The line of stitching appears unbroken on both sides.

QUESTIONS AND ANSWERS

Q. Do I need to knot off every time I stop?   *A.* It is all right to end a quilting session without knotting off the last thread. Just unthread the needle and leave the thread loose until the next session. Store the needle in a case of some kind—never a pincushion. Rethread a needle when ready to begin stitching again.

Q. Can I leave my needle in the quilt?   *A.* No. Batting attracts moisture and needles can rust.

Q. Can I leave my quilt in the hoop between sessions?   *A.* Take the quilt out of the hoop between stitching sessions. This removes the pressure from both the top and the batting.

Q. What color thread should be used on the quilt?   *A.* Whatever the quilter prefers—there is no "should" here. You can even use more than one color thread on one quilt.

Q. What should I do if I can't find quilting thread in a color I like?   *A.* Feel free to use a regular sewing thread. One with a polyester core should be strong enough. To make this type of thread stiffer and slicker, pull it through beeswax.

Q. What should I do if I keep bending my needle?   *A.* Try the next larger size (lower number). Hand needle sizes go from 1 to 12, with 1 being the largest and 12 the smallest.

Chapter 9

Machine Quilting

Even though machine-quilted pieces have existed for more than 100 years, machine quilting has been viewed as a less desirable process. This is no longer true, and machine enthusiasts welcome the recognition of this somewhat faster, but far from easier, technique. As does hand quilting, machine quilting requires attention to good tools and *practice*.

EQUIPMENT AND SETUP

Sewing Machine

The first step to successful machine quilting is the honest assessment of your sewing machine and its capabilities. The features you need are:

1. A strong, sound motor. Featherweights are not recommended.
2. Sufficient clearance between presser foot and throat plate. Some machines cannot accommodate the bulk of a quilt.
3. Even-feed capability. Some machines have this built in; most require an additional foot. Feet with teeth or rubber on the bottom are best; slick metal feet don't really aid in moving the quilt.
4. Darning capability. The machine should come with a darning foot, have one available by special order, or accept a generic model. Use of a spring needle is usually frustrating and unsuccessful.
5. Reliable, adjustable tension. The machine should accept various kinds of threads, including transparent nylon or polyester, without jamming. The tension should accept changes and return to the original setting without problems.
6. Feed dog versatility. The feed dogs can be dropped (preferable) or covered.
7. Small hole throat plate. This added attraction prevents the quilt from being pushed or drawn down into the wider slot of a zigzag throatplate, especially during free-motion quilting.

In reality, many sewing machine dealers are unfamiliar with machine quilting accessories. If at all possible, test the foot on *your* machine before leaving the store. Deal with any fit or quality problems right away.

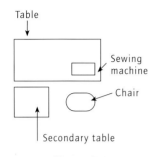

Figure 9.1

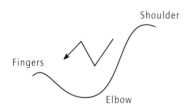

No

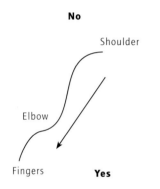

Yes

Figure 9.2

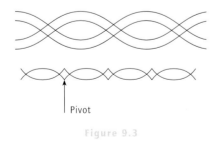

Figure 9.3

Workspace

The second step to success is choosing equipment and conditions that facilitate machine quilting:

1. Tables. A large table for the machine to sit on or, better yet, be set into, is a valuable aid. Set the machine toward the right end of the table, and put a smaller table at your left side to help hold the weight of the quilt as you work (fig. 9.1).
2. Chair. A chair with adjustable seat height and back support helps avoid back and shoulder problems.
3. Light source. Sewing machine lights are not overly bright, and any additional light shining on the bed of the machine is a great help.

Machine quilting is a very physical activity. You need to provide yourself with the best possible working conditions. If you hunch over the machine or feel as if you are constantly pushing the quilt up and over the machine bed, you will soon be a candidate for extensive chiropractic care. Ideally, the controlling motion of your hands on the quilt should begin at your shoulders and flow down your arms, through slightly bent elbows, to your fingers (fig. 9.2). This requires you to sit high in relation to your machine.

Several other hints may be useful. In addition to being certain that the machine is clean inside and properly lubricated, clean the machine bed. The quilt will slide with less effort over a clean surface. You may also find it helpful to lightly starch the backing fabric when you give it the final pressing. This helps the quilt pass more easily through the machine. Finally, you may wish to use rubber fingertips (from the business supply store). All this adds up to more traction for you and less for the quilt!

Just as with hand quilting, there is a rhythm to machine quilting. While this may apply more to free-motion quilting than to even-feed work, it is true that when you feel "in sync" with your tools, you are doing satisfying work. Set up your quilting area to serve you in this way.

Machine Feet

The third step is choosing the right machine feet. All types of hand quilting can be duplicated or approximated on the machine: in-the-ditch, gridwork, at the quarter inch, echo, meander, and outline.

The *even-feed foot* is used to stitch:

- in-the-ditch
- gridwork
- some outline work, such as gently curved or pivot-curved lines in a border or from edge to edge (fig. 9.3)

The *darning foot* can be used to do all types of quilting, even straight-line work. Most often it is used for these types of free-motion quilting:

- continuous line designs (outline)
- continuous curve
- echo
- stipple or meander quilting

QUILTING BY MACHINE

Stitch Length

The fourth step to successful machine quilting is handling the stitch length. For even-feed machine quilting, this is controlled by the feed dogs, as in usual machine sewing. Free-motion quilting does not use feed dogs. Therefore, the stitch length is controlled by two factors: (1) the speed at which the machine needle moves up and down, and (2) the speed at which your hands move the quilt under the needle.

The *needle-stop down feature* on a machine is helpful here. It allows you to stop your forward progress with the needle secure in the quilt. You do not have to take a hand off the quilt to turn the flywheel, so you can reposition your hands or the quilt, and begin stitching again with less chance of straying from the quilting design line.

I like the look of 10 stitches to the inch (4 stitches to the cm), which shows off the thread work nicely, allows for fairly tight curves without creating points in them, and doesn't perforate the quilt with too many small stitches.

Beginning and Ending

Begin or end a line of stitching based on its location. There are three basic choices:

1. If the stitching travels from edge to edge and will be covered by binding, begin outside one raw edge of the quilt and stitch past the opposite raw edge.
2. To hand finish a stitching line that begins and ends anywhere on the quilt, stitch the line of quilting from end to end, leaving 1½″ to 2″ (4cm to 5cm) of thread at each end. Turn the quilt over and use the bobbin thread to pull the top thread through to the back at both ends of the line. Knot the two threads together, and thread a basting darner with the two ends. Use it to pull them and the knot under the surface and into the batting layer; repeat.
3. To machine lock a stitching line using the even-feed foot (feed dogs are operating), begin the line with the stitch length set almost at 0 for seven or eight stitches, then reset the stitch length to quilting size. Continue at this setting until just before reaching the end of the line. Finish the stitching line by resetting the length to almost 0. These minuscule stitches hold the ends of the stitching line quite securely. *Carefully* trim the threads close to the first and last stitches.

To machine lock a free-motion stitching line (no feed dogs), make one stitch. Pull gently on the top thread to bring the bobbin thread to the surface. Place both threads to the side, out of the stitching line. Make several tiny stitches before beginning to move along the marked quilting line. At the end of the line, again make several tiny stitches. Clip the threads *carefully*.

It is easier to make smooth lines of stitching and consistent-size stitches by running the machine quickly. This will require some practice!

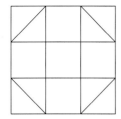

Figure 9.4

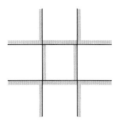

Figure 9.5

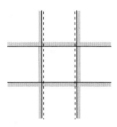

Figure 9.6

Figure 9.7

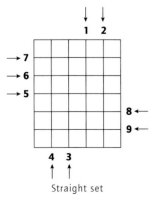

Straight set

Figure 9.8a

Practice Squares

The value of practice pieces cannot be overstated. Six practice squares will provide a taste of the machine quilting styles and help you perfect your technique before you tackle your quilt. To make the practice squares, cut and assemble the following:

Three 12½" (32cm) squares of plain muslin

One 12½" (32cm) square of a large floral print

One 12½" (32cm) *Nine-Patch* square: cut nine 4½" (11cm) squares; stitch together (consult Project 2 for assembly directions if needed)

One 12½" (32cm) *Shoo Fly* square: cut five 4½" (11cm) squares; four 4⅞" (12.5cm) squares, recut once on the diagonal to yield eight half-square triangles; stitch together, making the triangles into squares first, and then assemble like a *Nine-Patch* (fig. 9.4)

Six 16" (40cm) squares of plain muslin for backing

Six 16" (40cm) batting squares (use a variety of types, including the batt you plan to use for your "real" quilt)

Mark one of the plain muslin squares with small continuous line designs such as vines, cables, or swags. Mark one plain muslin square in the center with an 8" (20cm) diameter continuous line design. Check the Bibliography for design sources.

Using the Even-Feed Foot

Preparation: even-feed foot on the machine

           stitch length set to 10 stitches to the inch (4 stitches to the cm)

           bobbin thread—cotton or cotton-wrapped polyester core

           top thread—machine quilting or transparent (try both)

Stitch in-the-Ditch

Used on virtually every machine-quilted project, these are the lines of quilting that anchor the quilt sandwich. Use the *Nine-Patch* practice block. Find which direction the seams have been pressed (fig. 9.5).

The lines of quilting are stitched on the seamline side opposite the pressed seam allowances. Begin with the longest lines (fig. 9.6). As you stitch, the needle rides just barely (2 to 3 threads) to the side of the seamline. Note where the needle is in relation to the front of the foot. This will help you to guide the quilt under the foot.

Remember to glance ahead as you stitch. As Harriet Hargrave, machine quilting authority, says, it's like driving a car. You will steer much better if you look down the road, rather than only at the hood ornament. You are prepared for what is coming.

To stitch the seamlines where the pressed seam changes position, the needle will do the same. A very small motion will carry the needle to the other side of the seamline at the joint (fig. 9.7). If the batting is puffy, it may make it easier to see the seam if you spread the fabric slightly. Do this by exerting gentle pressure with both hands away from the seam as it passes under the foot. When you are about to cross a previous line of machine stitching, you may see the fabric begin to bunch as you approach the line. Use your fingertips to push this fabric *toward* the even-feed foot. The foot will ease in the fabric bubble by the time you reach the stitching to be crossed.

Since there is a finite amount of space under the arm of the ordinary home sewing machine, always put the least amount of quilt through that space. Begin stitching at the middle of the quilt and progress to the edge (moving the bulk of the quilt always to your left, out from under the machine arm). Rotate the quilt 180° and stitch again, center to edge. Rotate the quilt 90°, stitch. Rotate the quilt 180°, stitch. This procedure is identical for blocks set straight or on point (fig. 9.8a–b). Roll the edge of the quilt that passes under the arm, reducing its bulk as much as possible (fig. 9.9).

As you work on these practice blocks, rotate and stitch them just as if you were working on a large quilt. When you start your real work, the practice will prove valuable.

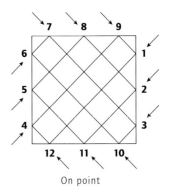

On point

Figure 9.8b

Figure 9.9

Stitch Gridwork

Using the same *Nine-Patch* block, practice some gridwork. Stitch diagonally across the block twice from corner to corner. These lines can be marked with chalk or a crease made by a Hera marker. Or try stitching by "eyeballing" the line—no marks, just using the seam joints and block corners to guide the needle (fig. 9.10). To stitch additional lines, use one of two methods:

1. Mark lines at 1½" (4cm) intervals, parallel to the center diagonals; stitch on the lines (fig. 9.11).
2. Use a bar that fastens to the even-feed foot and can be set at various distances to guide the needle. Align the bar with one diagonal row, measuring so the needle will stitch 1½" (4cm) to the right of the bar (fig. 9.12). Tighten the bar in place. Stitch the line while the bar rides along the original diagonal row of stitching. Repeat, aligning the bar with the last row stitched.

Try doing gridwork on other plain blocks, with variations in line widths. Use more than one thread color or try variegated thread for different effects.

Remember that the even-feed foot can also be used to create undulating lines across the quilt surface; gentle curved lines, such as some cables; and curved lines with pivot points (see fig. 9.3). The even-feed foot is not designed to make tight curves and circles. These lines are better executed using free-motion stitching.

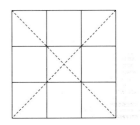

Figure 9.10

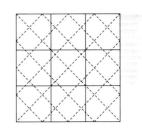

Figure 9.11

Using the Darning Foot

Free-motion stitching is much like figure skating. When it's good, it's wonderful! When it's awkward, uneven, and poorly executed, it's awful. Free-motion stitching takes practice. But think of all the useful dog and cat blankets or doll quilts you can make to donate to good causes while you practice!

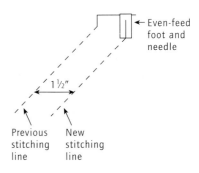

Figure 9.12

Preparation: darning foot attached to machine
feed dogs lowered or covered
bobbin thread—cotton or cotton-wrapped polyester core
top thread—machine quilting or transparent (try both)

Free-Motion Stitching

The unmarked muslin square is your doodle cloth. Use this to get the feel of stitching with the darning foot. (Not unlike working without a net!) This foot functions in tandem with the needle. Remember to engage the presser foot lever: the tension disks are not engaged unless the lever is down. The darning foot sits rather high and does not hold the quilt tight to the machine bed. Because of this, it is easy to think that the presser foot lever is engaged when in reality it is not. Practice stitching in all directions on this block. Stitch across from left to right and then from right to left. Stitch toward your body and away from it.

Designate a "north" for your doodle cloth. Always keep that at the top as you practice stitching. Do not turn the block. You cannot turn an entire quilt in circles under the arm of the machine, so don't practice that way.

Stitch with both machine quilting thread and transparent thread. Check the tension. Does it need to be adjusted for various threads? Make small changes, checking the thread on both sides of the block after each change.

Free-motion designs contain many curves and points. Use the practice configurations shown (fig. 9.13). Stitch in all directions (fig. 9.14). The secret to a good curve is to not stop while stitching it. Keep moving smoothly. The secret to a good point is to hesitate momentarily at the point—stitch up to it; hesitate for a stitch; then change direction, stitching out of it.

Try writing the alphabet or your name in lower case script. Note that in some places you will stitch back over what you stitched previously. That's fine and to be expected.

Practice moving the needle and the quilt quickly and smoothly in all directions. Use your fingers to hold and guide the quilt under the needle. You will begin to find a comfortable speed for both. It will feel right and the stitches will begin to look consistent. Your fingers need to get quite close to the foot to give the greatest control. There is also a new horseshoe-shaped hoop that you might like to try. The small darning rings that come with some sewing machines are not suitable for quilting.

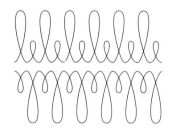

Figure 9.13

Continuous Line Stitching

Now try stitching the marked lines of the continuous line design sample. Remember to practice beginning and ending the threads. Before starting to stitch any design, it's a good idea to give it a "dry run." Place the design under the darning foot and, without lowering the foot or using the needle, move the quilt along, keeping the line properly oriented to the needle. This shows you when to move forward or back, left or right (fig. 9.15). Don't turn the block! After you practice each design, stitch it.

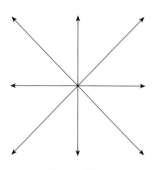

Figure 9.14

Continuous Line and Echo Stitching

Use the larger and more involved continuous line design for the center of this practice square. Stitch the design. Don't turn the block!

To echo the outside edge of the design, measure and mark the first echo line. I like the first line at ½" (1.5cm) and successive ones at ¼" (0.75cm). You may do it that way, or use your darning foot as a measure and stitch at that width (fig. 9.16). Practice several echo lines. Remember to strive for smooth curves, clean points, and consistent stitches.

Figure 9.15   Figure 9.16

Continuous Curve Stitching

Use the *Shoo Fly* block to practice this machine facsimile of stitching at the quarter inch. The stitching line makes gentle arcs within each pieced shape. These arcs extend no more than ¼" (0.75cm) into the shape at the deepest part of the curve. You may choose to mark these curves with a template, or to put a mark at the spot where the center of each curve should be. Another option is to use the edges of the darning foot against the seams as a guide. After you've practiced these maneuvers, you probably won't need to mark at all. Again, you will find a rhythm for this style of quilting.

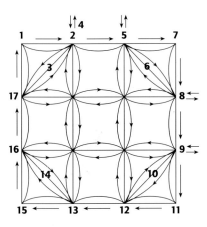

Figure 9.17

Begin at one corner of the block (upper left is usual, but it really doesn't matter). Study the diagram and then "dry run" the block (fig. 9.17). You might want to do this step several times. When ready, stitch the continuous curves on the piecework. Work toward smooth curves and consistent stitches.

Outline Stitching

Stitching around some printed shapes can be a fast, lovely way to accent the fabric. Don't try to stitch on every line. Look at your block and select large shapes and some of the lines within the shapes. For example, don't stitch around every petal of a large, complex flower; stitch around the outside edge and a few interior shapes.

Find large areas to highlight in the block. Try to find "paths," such as vines or stems, that allow you to stitch into and out of these areas. This is a good place to experiment with transparent thread.

Stippling or Meander Stitching

To give texture to background areas, use stippling or meander quilting. These wandering lines of quilting look somewhat like jigsaw puzzle pieces. The more closely the lines are packed into an area, the flatter the quilted look. This stitch can be used effectively to make other less-quilted areas puff up.

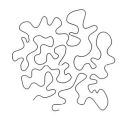

Figure 9.18

Meander lines of stitching do not cross each other, do not have any sharp corners, do not line up into rows, and do not appear to have a beginning or end (fig. 9.18).

Stabilizing the Quilt

Once you have tried these styles of machine quilting, you can apply them to any of the projects in this book, or to your own creations. Stabilize any quilt by first stitching in-the-ditch of both the horizontal and vertical seams. Then add additional even-feed or free-motion stitching. Plan the quilting to be well distributed over the entire surface. A good test is to make a fist and set it down anywhere on the quilt. If your fist doesn't touch a line of quilting, more is needed.

Rolling the quilt through the machine is a challenge—another of the good reasons to start small. Roll or pleat the quilt neatly from the side to the middle, as compactly as is reasonable without totally smashing the batting. Just remember to keep moving the bulk of the quilt to the left, out from under the machine arm, each time you move to a new stitching line.

The last part of this process is to stabilize the outside edge of the quilt. Stitch at ³⁄₁₆″ (0.5cm) around the perimeter, using the even-feed foot and a long stitch length, or hand baste. At this time, all pins should be removed from the quilt, but do not trim the edge now. This will be done after the binding has been stitched in place.

Chapter 10

Binding

The basic edge finish for a quilt is the *binding*, which protects the edges from wear and tear, and provides a smooth, clean look. Adding the binding is the final stage in completing your quilt.

MAKING THE BINDING STRIPS

Check the perimeter of the quilt by laying it flat. Are the sides straight and do the corners form a 90° angle? If a side is slightly wobbly, some correction is possible in the application of the binding. Using a long *straight* edge, such as a yardstick, mark a chalk or pencil line to show the corrected outside edge. If a corner is slightly out of square, also mark the correct 90° angle. A square rotary ruler is very useful here. Measure or calculate the perimeter width; make at least 10″ (25cm) more binding than you need.

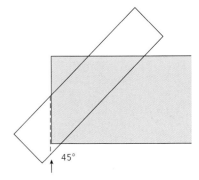

Figure 10.1

To make the binding, cut bias or cross-grain strips of fabric. For a narrow binding, cut these strips at 2¼″ (5.5cm). For a slightly wider binding, cut the strips at 2½″ (6.5cm). I prefer bias binding because I like the way it turns corners. It is also supposed to better handle wear and tear on the edge of the quilt. Some quilters prefer to apply straight (cross-grain) binding. Try both and decide which is more comfortable for you to work with.

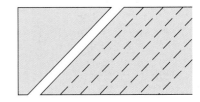

Figure 10.2

To cut bias strips, set the 45° angle of the rotary ruler parallel to a selvage edge of the fabric, and cut along the edge of the ruler (fig. 10.1). Cut lengths of bias, placing the measurement line for the desired width, 2¼″ or 2½″ (5.5cm or 6.5cm), against the previously cut edge (fig. 10.2). Cut at least one length of bias from the triangle pieces left at each end of the fabric (fig. 10.3). Cut cross-grain strips in the same way as for piecework. These are used to make straight binding.

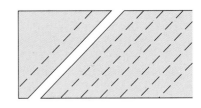

Figure 10.3

Now trim both ends of each bias or cross-grain strip to a clean 45° angle. Lay out each strip, one at a time and right side up, in front of you on the rotary mat. Using a smaller ruler, place the 45° line at the top of the binding strip and trim the left end along the edge of the ruler. Keeping the ruler in the same position, move it to the other end of the strip, and trim the right end (fig. 10.4).

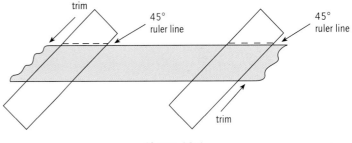

Figure 10.4

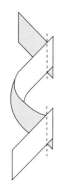

Figure 10.5

Stack the strips, right sides up, and take them to the sewing machine. You can also stitch these together by hand, should you so desire. Follow the diagram to stitch all of the binding strips into one long piece (fig. 10.5).

Press the seams open on the wrong side. Then, with *wrong* sides together, press the strip in half along its entire length. Don't stretch it. It is now ready to apply to the edges of the quilt, using the even-feed foot.

ATTACHING THE BINDING

You may begin on any edge; I usually start on the bottom of the quilt. Place the cut double edge of the binding against the outside edge of the quilt (or against the line indicating the corrected edge of the quilt). The fold of the binding is toward the middle of the quilt. Leaving at least 10″ (25cm) of binding unsewn, begin to stitch a ¼″ (0.75cm) seam near the middle of this side—called Side 1 (fig. 10.6). Use a stitch length of at least 12 to the inch (5 to the cm). As you approach the first corner, stop stitching for a moment. Measure and mark the binding at ¼″ (0.75cm) from the corner. Continue stitching until you reach the mark; backstitch (fig. 10.7). Move the quilt out from under the even-feed foot and turn it, so that Side 1 is now at the top.

Pick up the binding at the corner, and fold the loose end up over the stitched end, causing the binding to form a 45° angle (fig. 10.8). Now fold the loose end back down, with the cut edge of the binding along the next quilt edge to be stitched. Make the fold even with the edge of Side 1 and begin stitching Side 2 from the edge of the fold (fig. 10.9).

Continue stitching Side 2; measure and mark the ¼″ (0.75cm); stitch to the mark; backstitch; turn the corner. Stitch Side 3 and Side 4, turning the corner to take you back to Side 1 (fig. 10.10). Begin stitching Side 1 and sew 3″ to 4″ (7cm to 10cm). Stop, cut the threads, and take the quilt out from under the even-feed foot.

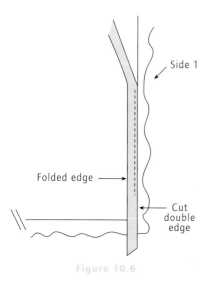

Side 1

Folded edge ——→

←— Cut double edge

Figure 10.6

Joining the Ends

Place the quilt on a flat surface and straighten out the two loose ends of binding, opening up the fold and laying the pieces flat, one on top of the other. It is very important to get everything absolutely flat—both the quilt and the binding ends. Follow the diagrams to mark (pin and check), cut, and stitch the ends of the binding together (fig. 10.11 a–e). You may wish to briefly change presser feet to do this stitching. Using the ¼″ (0.75cm) foot makes it easier to see the Vs at the top and bottom of the joining seam and to stitch straight through them. Put the even-feed foot back on before continuing.

Align the joined binding back along the edge of Side 1 and stitch it in place, making certain that the seam along Side 1 is complete.

Place the quilt flat again. Check the edges. Are they straight? If so, move on to trimming the edges. If not, adjust the binding.

To trim the edges of the quilt if you have used 2¼″ (5.5cm) binding, place the ¼″ (0.75cm) line of the long rotary ruler along the binding seam. The edge of the ruler will just skim the cut edge of the binding. *Carefully* trim away the

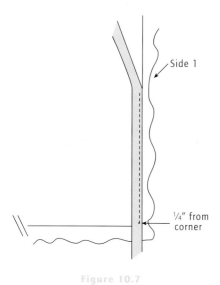

Side 1

¼″ from corner

Figure 10.7

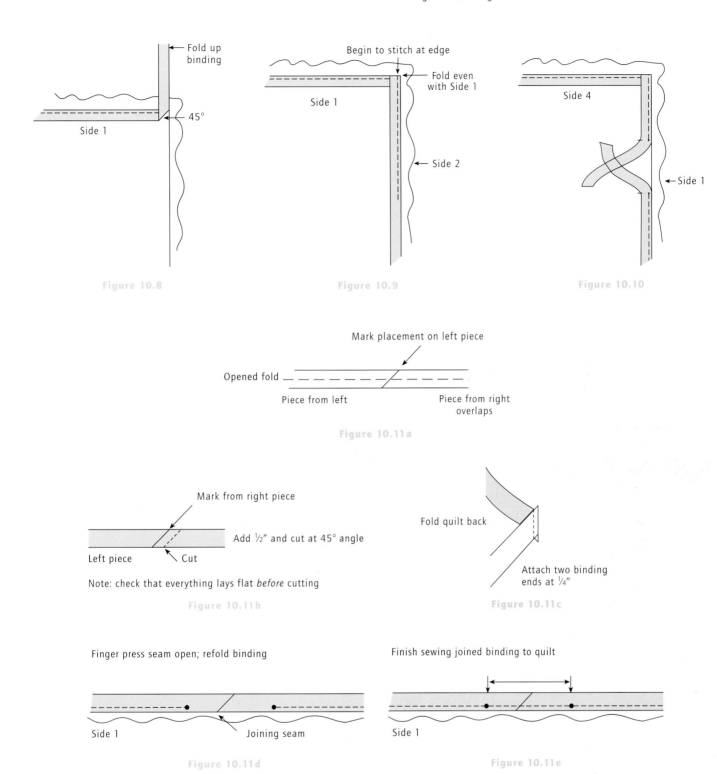

Fold up binding

45°

Side 1

Figure 10.8

Begin to stitch at edge

Fold even with Side 1

Side 1

Side 2

Figure 10.9

Side 4

Side 1

Figure 10.10

Mark placement on left piece

Opened fold

Piece from left

Piece from right overlaps

Figure 10.11a

Mark from right piece

Add ½" and cut at 45° angle

Left piece   Cut

Note: check that everything lays flat *before* cutting

Figure 10.11b

Fold quilt back

Attach two binding ends at ¼"

Figure 10.11c

Finger press seam open; refold binding

Side 1   Joining seam

Figure 10.11d

Finish sewing joined binding to quilt

Side 1

Figure 10.11e

excess batting and backing using the rotary cutter. *Do not* let the rotary cutter slice the fold of the binding at the corners!

Having read that caution, you will know why I prefer the 2½" (6.5cm) binding. With this binding, place the ⅜" (1cm) line of the rotary ruler along the binding seam and trim. This size gives me a slightly wider binding and more room in the trimming.

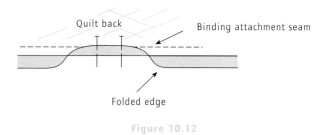

Figure 10.12

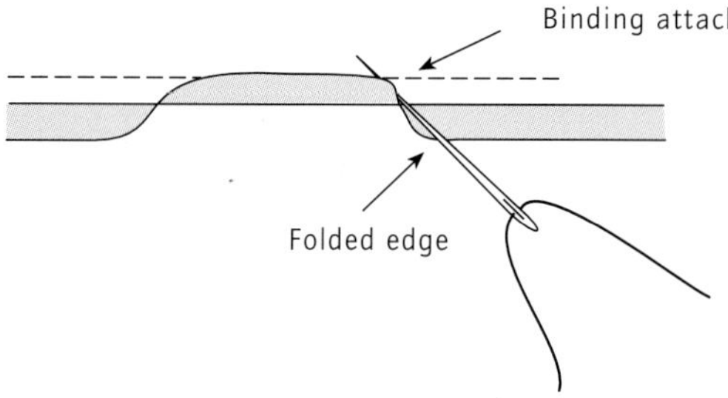

Figure 10.13

Finishing the Binding

The binding should look and feel full of batting as you turn it and stitch it down. Select a thread that will blend with the binding, a sturdy sharp needle, a thimble (optional), and several pins. Turn the folded edge of the binding to the back, up and over the line of stitching, and secure 3" to 4" (7cm to 10cm) of it with several pins (fig. 10.12). I don't pin very much of the binding down at one time, because I don't want to constantly snag the thread or scratch myself.

Cut an 18" (45cm) length of thread, thread the needle, and put a small knot at the end. Insert the needle and single thread into the trimmed edge of the quilt and bring it up through the fold of the binding (fig. 10.13). Blind stitch the binding to the back of the quilt, taking care not to stitch through onto the front of the quilt. Make small stitches, about ³⁄₁₆" (0.25cm) apart, pulling the edge of the binding snug to the backing.

To turn a corner, slightly trim across the corner of the quilt; trim the top, batting, and backing, *not the binding*, at a 45° angle. Stitch up to the seam at the corner, with the binding folded up beyond the corner (fig. 10.14) and take two stitches to secure the side. Then fold the binding up toward the seam on the next side, making a 45° angle at the corner (fig. 10.15). If it seems too bulky, carefully trim away a little more of the quilt.

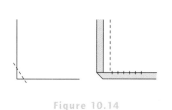

Figure 10.14

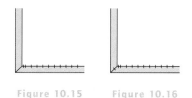

Figure 10.15   Figure 10.16

Don't forget to sign and date your work. You may approach it like a painter and stitch this information into the front of your quilt. Or you may decide to make a label for the back. Another idea is to incorporate the label (as a decorated square or rectangle of cloth) right into the backing or the hanging sleeve.

Labels may be as plain or informative as you wish. Sometimes they simply state the quiltmaker's name, place of residence, and the quilt's date of completion. Others are decorated with pen drawings and tell a whole story about the quilt. Whatever your choice, just be certain to document your special quilt.

To hold the binding corner fold in place, slip the needle halfway down the binding toward the corner point and catch-stitch both folds, front and back (fig. 10.16). Then return the needle to the binding fold and stitch down the side. Continue around the quilt, turning each corner in the same manner. I used to avoid doing the binding years ago when I began quilting, because I truly didn't know how easy it was to make a good-looking one. Now I really enjoy putting a crisp, clean finish on my work. You will feel the same satisfaction, I'm sure.

Congratulations! You've made a quilt. May this be the first of many to bring joy to you and the lucky people with whom you share them. The fundamentals you have learned will provide a solid base for all of your quiltmaking adventures. I hope this book will continue to be a useful companion. Be open to new or different ideas and techniques. Incorporate what works for you. Above all, enjoy both the "doing" and the result. Happy stitching!

Appendix 1
Sampler Quilts

Use the two sampler quilts to practice piecing, appliqué, and quilting techniques. All essential quiltmaking skills are reinforced through the variety of blocks. Either quilt is ideal for use by teachers who offer a four- to six-week class in beginning quiltmaking.

Project 13

Buckskin Sunset

60" × 73" (152cm × 185cm)

Lynn G. Kough, Chandler, Arizona ◆ machine pieced; machine quilted

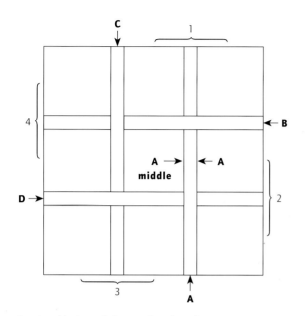

Sew two blocks and short sashes, four times.
A: partial seams joining center block and pair 2
B: join B and block pair 1
C: join C and block pair 4
D: join D and block pair 3
A: finish A seams

Here is a small challenge for you—another step in your growth as a quiltmaker. The nine blocks for this quilt finish at 12″ (30cm) square. *Grandma's Star, Blackford's Beauty,* and *LeMoyne Star* are 12″ (30cm) blocks in the projects in Chapter 4. Remembering how block sizes are calculated based on a grid, what is the finished size of the *Nine-Patch* square for a 12″ (30cm) block? If you said 4″ (10cm), give yourself a pat on the back. How about the large triangle in *Birds in the Air*? What is the length of its leg? The correct answer is 6″ (16cm). Good! Now calculate the sizes of the *Ohio Star* pieces.

The background block for the project size of *Chrysanthemum* is 10½″ (27cm), unfinished. What size block will you cut for this quilt? Templates are given for the *Drunkard's Path* in this 12″ (30cm) size. Cut the *Courthouse Steps* as follows (includes seam allowances):

A and **B** 2½″ × 2½″ (6.5cm × 6.5cm)
C and **D** 2½″ × 6½″ (6.5cm × 16.5cm)
E   2½″ × 10½″ (6.5cm × 26.5cm)
F   1½″ × 10½″ (4cm × 26.5cm)
G   1½″ × 12½″ (4cm × 36.5cm)

The "fusion" of 60° triangle-based designs—*Tumbling Blocks, Inner City, Texas Star,* and *Thousand Pyramids*—uses the same templates given for Project 8.

The sashing for the nine blocks looks as if it were woven. Remember how you finished the *Tumbling Blocks* project with partial seams? The same trick will work here. The diagram shows the order in which the units are sewn together if you wish to try this. Have fun—I did!

Finished Sizes

Finished blocks	nine 12″ (30cm)
Finished section	10″ × 42″ (25cm × 106cm)
Finished sashing	3″ (7.5cm) wide
Finished inner border	3″ (7.5cm) wide
Finished outer border	6″ (16cm) wide
Backing	64″ × 77″ (165cm × 200cm)
Binding	7½ yds. (6.8m)

Fabric Requirements

Blocks	two packs of eight ¼ yards, hand-dyed fabrics (or 16 quarters)
Sashing	one pack of four ¼ yards, hand-dyed fabrics (or 4 quarters)
Inner border	⅔ yd. (0.6m)
Outer border	1¾ yds. (1.7m)
Backing	3¼ yds. (2.9m)
Binding	¾ yd. (0.7m)
Batting	72″ × 90″ (185cm × 230cm)

Hot Tropic Hearts

44″ × 44″ (112cm × 112cm); 4 blocks on point; setting triangles; sashing; 1 plain border

Lynn G. Kough, Chandler, Arizona ◆ machine appliquéd; machine quilted

And here's your appliqué challenge! Use one template; make it smaller and/or larger; arrange the pieces in sprays, rings, layers—whatever! The three-part template I used is given. Can you see how the sashing is fitted to the blocks using corner squares? I'll leave it up to you to choose straight seam or mitered borders. You know how to do both! Your template could be a leaf, circle, fish, bird, diamond, apple, flower . . . the possibilities are endless!

Finished Sizes

Finished blocks	four 10″ (25cm) squares
Finished sashing	2″ (5cm) wide
Setting triangles	8
Finished border	5″ (12.7cm) wide
Backing	48″ (122cm) square
Binding	5 yds. (6m)

Fabric Requirements

Hearts	¼ yd. (0.2m) *each* of three fabrics
Background	1⅛ yds. (1.1m)
Sashing	⅜ yd. (0.3m)
Border	¾ yd. (0.7m)
Backing	1⅔ yds. (1.5m)
Binding	½ yd. (0.5m)
Batting	45″ × 60″ (115cm × 155cm)

Appendix 2

Resources

You may find the following products useful in your quiltmaking.

Appliqué pressing sheets. For bonding fabrics to fusibles, appliqué nonstick pressing sheets are great tools. They keep the adhesive off your iron and ironing board.

For arranging fused fabric shapes before adhering them to the background block, the Appliqué Pressing Sheet™ is just about the best thing since sliced bread! Place this heavier transparent sheet over the pattern, arrange the shapes (overlapping) to match the pattern placement, and press them to the sheet. Allow them to cool and then lift the entire group of shapes off the sheet. Put them on the background block and fuse in place.

Safety pin closers. A product called Kwik Klip™ is a real hand saver. An ordinary grapefruit spoon can also be used to close safety pins by pressing down the serrated bowl on the top of the pin.

Rotary cutting tools. Projects 2, 5—Easy Set™ by Sharon Hultgren. This tool allows you to cut corner and setting triangles from fabric strips. It is sized for blocks from 30" to 120" (00cm to 00cm).

Projects 3, 4—Point Trimmer by Judy Martin. With this tool you eliminate dog ears and make it easier to align shapes when machine piecing.

Projects 3, 6—Easy Angle™ by Sharon Hultgren; Omnigrid ruler no. 96. These tools make it possible to cut many different sizes of right (90°) triangles (half-square triangles) from a strip of fabric, eliminating the need to cut and recut squares.

Projects 4, 6—Companion Angle™ by Darlene Zimmerman; Omnigrid ruler no. 98. These tools make it possible to cut many different sizes of quarter-square triangles from a strip of fabric, eliminating the need to cut and recut squares.

Project 5—Tri-Recs™ by Darlene Zimmerman and Joy Hoffman. For rotary cutting split-square shapes, this tool not only allows you to use strips of fabric, but also gives you the angle necessary to correctly align the two side triangles to the center triangle when machine piecing.

Projects 6, 7, 8—Quilter's Quarter Marker ™. This tool is handy for marking all different types of joint points when working with set-ins.

Project 10—EZ Dresden Plate Quilting Template. This guide was used to make both the *Chrysanthemum* and *Fan* templates.

Bibliography

DRAFTING, CUTTING, AND BLOCK DESIGNS

Beyer, Jinny. *The Quilter's Album of Blocks and Borders*. McLean, Va.: EPM Publications, Inc., 1986.

Johnson-Srebro, Nancy. *Measure the Possibilities with Omnigrid*. Burlington, Wash.: Omnigrid, Inc., 1993.

Martin, Judy. *Judy Martin's Ultimate Book of Quilt Block Patterns*. Grinnell, Iowa: Crosley-Griffith Publishing Co., 1990.

Wolfrom, Joen. *Make Any Block Any Size*. Lafayette, Calif.: C & T Publishing, 1999.

COLOR AND FABRIC

Beyer, Jinny. *Color Confidence for Quilters*. Lincolnwood (Chicago), Ill.: The Quilt Digest Press, 1992.

Hargrave, Harriet. *From Fiber to Fabric*. Lafayette, Calif.: C & T Publishing, 1997.

Horton, Roberta. *An Amish Adventure*. Lafayette, Calif.: C & T Publishing, 1983.

———. *Calico and Beyond: The Use of Patterned Fabric in Quilts*. Lafayette, Calif.: C & T Publishing, 1986.

———. *Plaids and Stripes*. Lafayette, Calif.: C & T Publishing, 1990.

Penders, Mary Coyne. *Color and Cloth*. Lincolnwood (Chicago), Ill.: The Quilt Digest Press, 1989.

APPLIQUÉ AND PIECEWORK

Hargrave, Harriet. *Mastering Machine Appliqué*. Lafayette, Calif.: C & T Publishing, 1991.

McCloskey, Marsha. *Lessons in Machine Piecing*. Bothell, Wash.: That Patchwork Place, 1990.

McClun, Diana, and Laura Nownes. *Quilts! Quilts!! Quilts!!!*, second edition, Lincolnwood (Chicago) Ill.: The Quilt Digest Press, 1997.

Sienkiewicz, Elly. *Baltimore Beauties and Beyond*, vol. 1. Lafayette, Calif.: C & T Publishing, 1989.

Sinema, Laurene. *Applique! Applique!! Applique!!!* Lincolnwood (Chicago) Ill.: The Quilt Digest Press, 1992.

SETTINGS AND BORDERS

Hanson, Joan. *Sensational Settings*. Bothell, Wash.: That Patchwork Place, 1993.

Martin, Judy, and Marsha McCloskey. *Pieced Borders: The Complete Resource*. Grinnell, Iowa: Crosley-Griffith Publishing Co., Inc., 1994.

QUILTING

Hargrave, Harriet. *Heirloom Machine Quilting*. Lafayette, Calif.: C & T Publishing, 1990.

Marston, Gwen, and Joe Cunningham. *Quilting with Style: Principles for Great Pattern Design*. Paducah, Ken.: American Quilter's Society, 1993.

McElroy, Roxanne. *That Perfect Stitch*. Lincolnwood (Chicago), Ill.: The Quilt Digest Press, 1997.

Noble, Maurine. *Machine Quilting Made Easy!* Bothell, Wash.: That Patchwork Place, 1994.

FINISHING

Dietrich, Mimi. *Happy Endings: Finishing the Edges of Your Quilt*. Bothell, Wash.: That Patchwork Place, 1987.

Mazuran, Cody. *A Fine Finish*. Bothell, Wash.: That Patchwork Place, 1997.

McKelvey, Susan. *A Treasury of Quilt Labels*. Lafayette, Calif.: C & T Publishing, 1993.

Courthouse
Steps

B

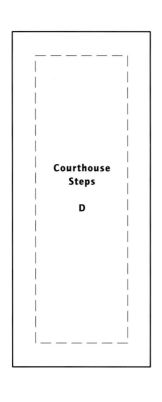

Courthouse
Steps

D

Courthouse
Steps

A

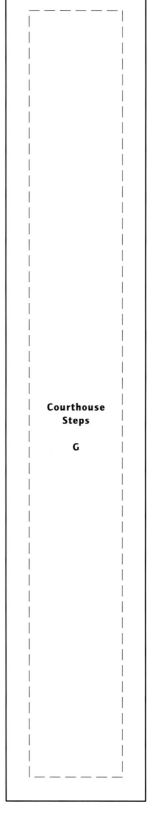

Courthouse
Steps

G

Courthouse
Steps

E

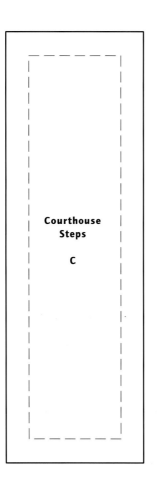

Courthouse
Steps

C

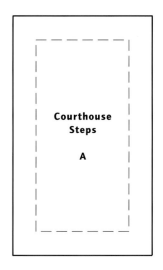

Courthouse
Steps

F

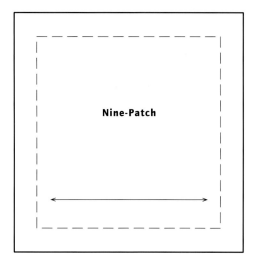

Nine-Patch

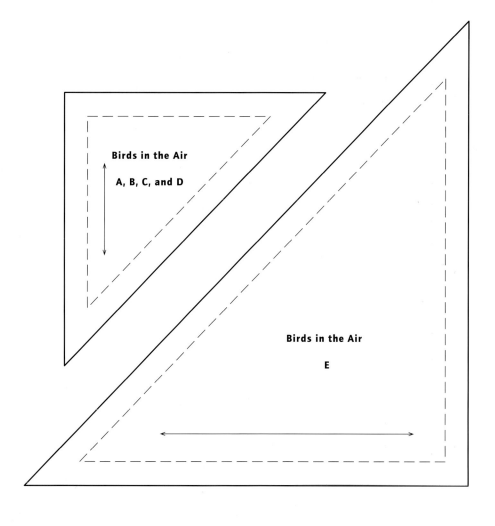

Birds in the Air

A, B, C, and D

Birds in the Air

E

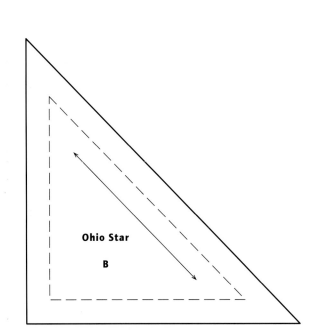

Ohio Star

B

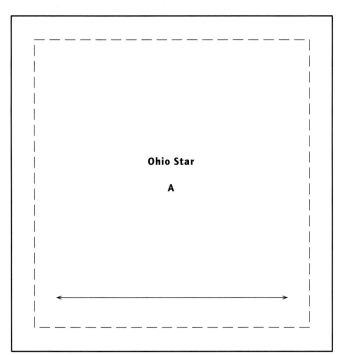

Ohio Star

A

Hot Tropic Hearts

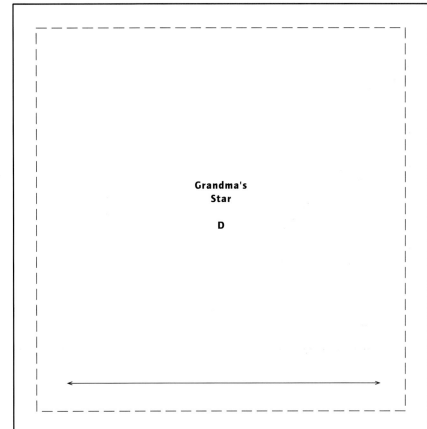

Grandma's
Star

D

Grandma's
Star

A

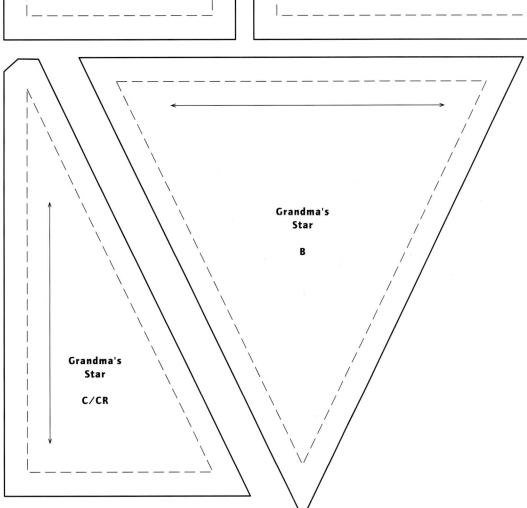

Grandma's
Star

B

Grandma's
Star

C/CR

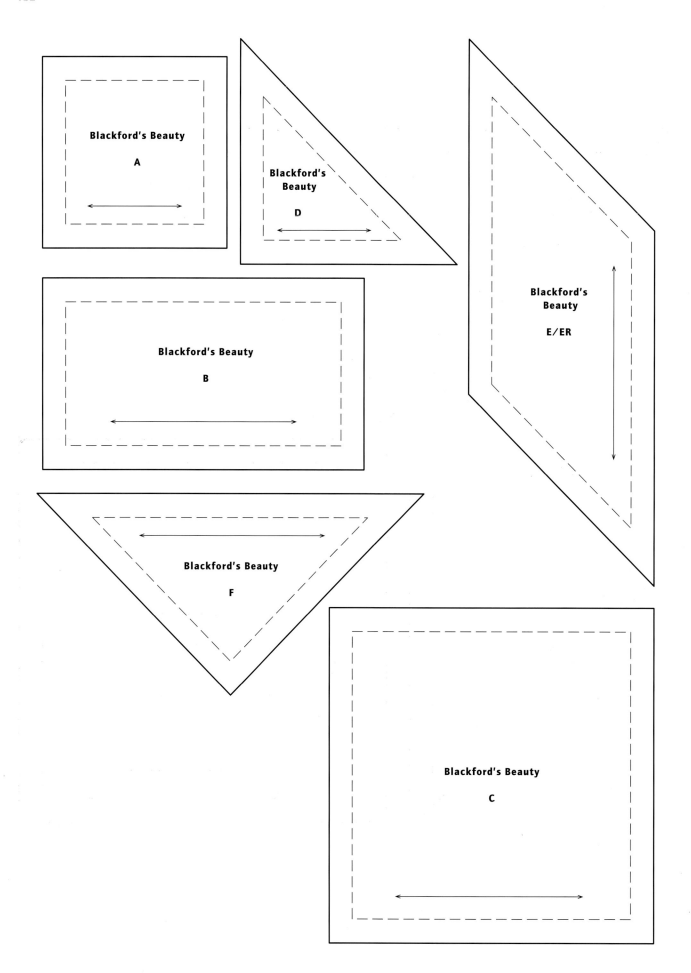

Blackford's Beauty
A

Blackford's Beauty
D

Blackford's Beauty
E/ER

Blackford's Beauty
B

Blackford's Beauty
F

Blackford's Beauty
C

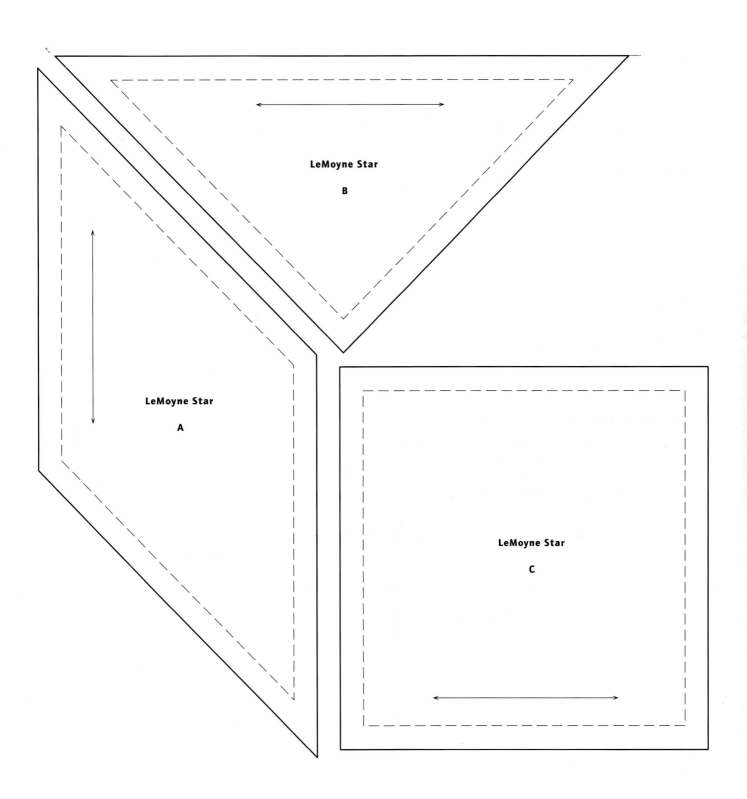

LeMoyne Star

B

LeMoyne Star

A

LeMoyne Star

C

134

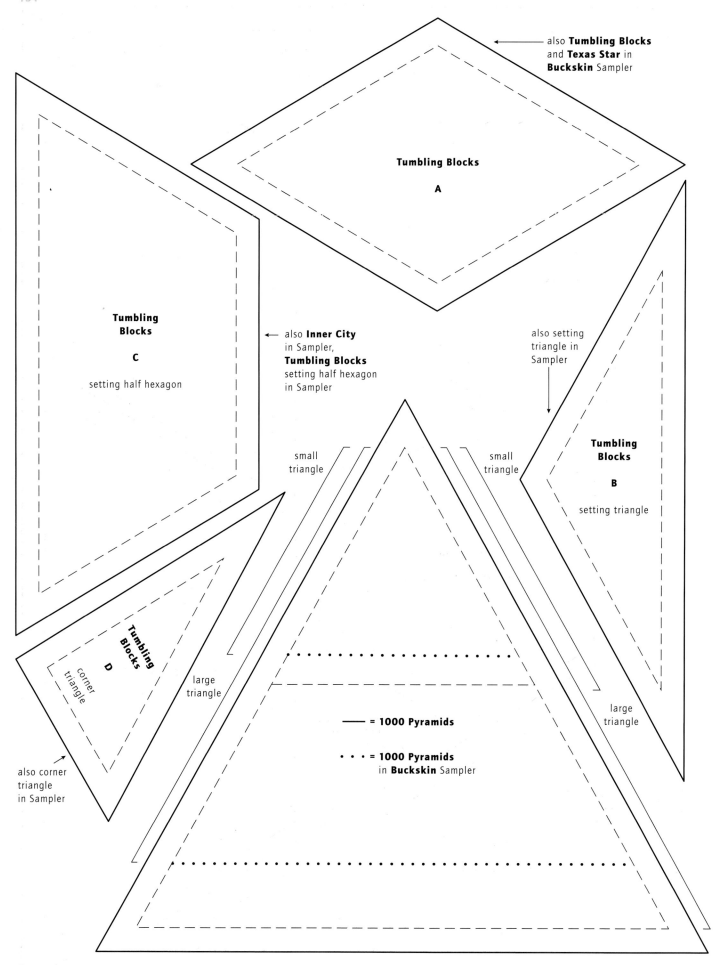

also **Tumbling Blocks**
and **Texas Star** in
Buckskin Sampler

Tumbling Blocks

A

Tumbling Blocks

C

setting half hexagon

also **Inner City**
in Sampler,
Tumbling Blocks
setting half hexagon
in Sampler

also setting
triangle in
Sampler

Tumbling Blocks

B

setting triangle

small
triangle

small
triangle

Tumbling Blocks

D

corner
triangle

large
triangle

large
triangle

—— = 1000 Pyramids

• • • = 1000 Pyramids
in **Buckskin** Sampler

also corner
triangle
in Sampler

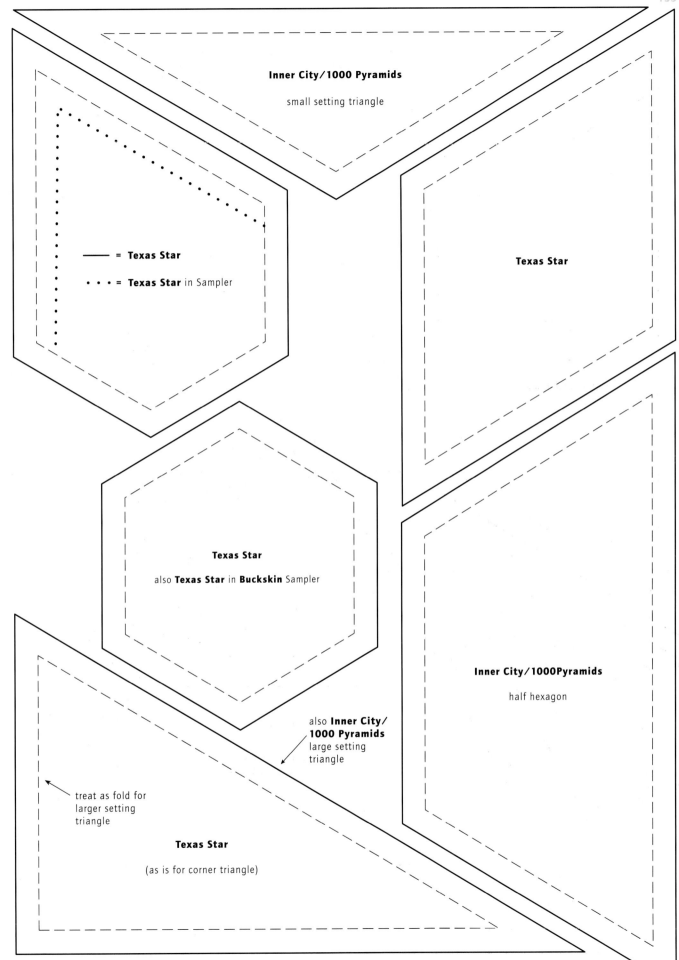

Inner City/1000 Pyramids

small setting triangle

―――― = **Texas Star**

• • • • = **Texas Star** in Sampler

Texas Star

Texas Star

also **Texas Star** in **Buckskin** Sampler

Inner City/1000Pyramids

half hexagon

also **Inner City/ 1000 Pyramids** large setting triangle

treat as fold for larger setting triangle

Texas Star

(as is for corner triangle)

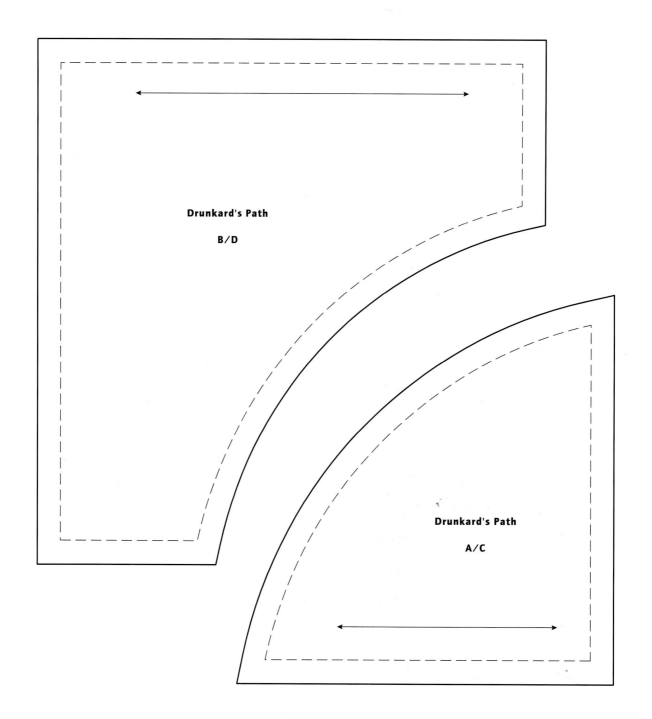

Drunkard's Path

B/D

Drunkard's Path

A/C

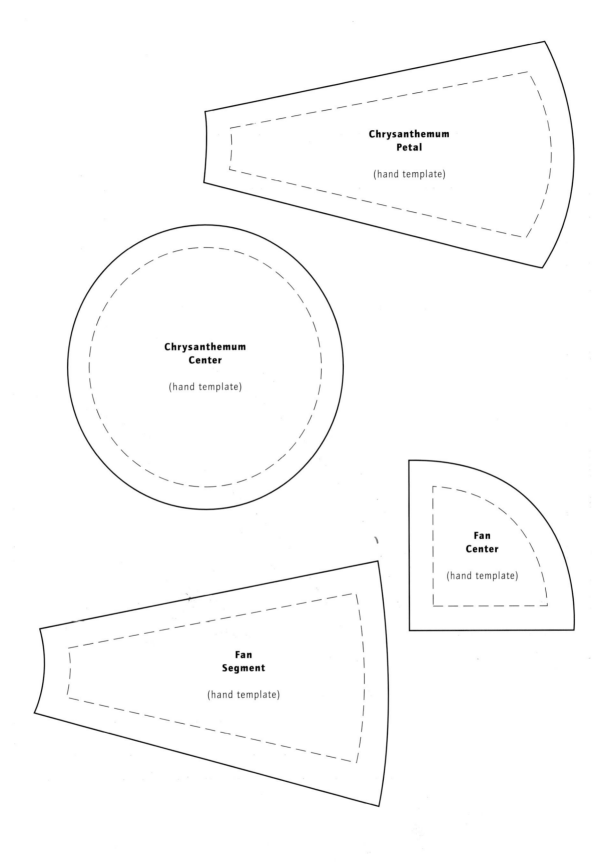

Chrysanthemum Petal

(hand template)

Chrysanthemum Center

(hand template)

Fan Center

(hand template)

Fan Segment

(hand template)

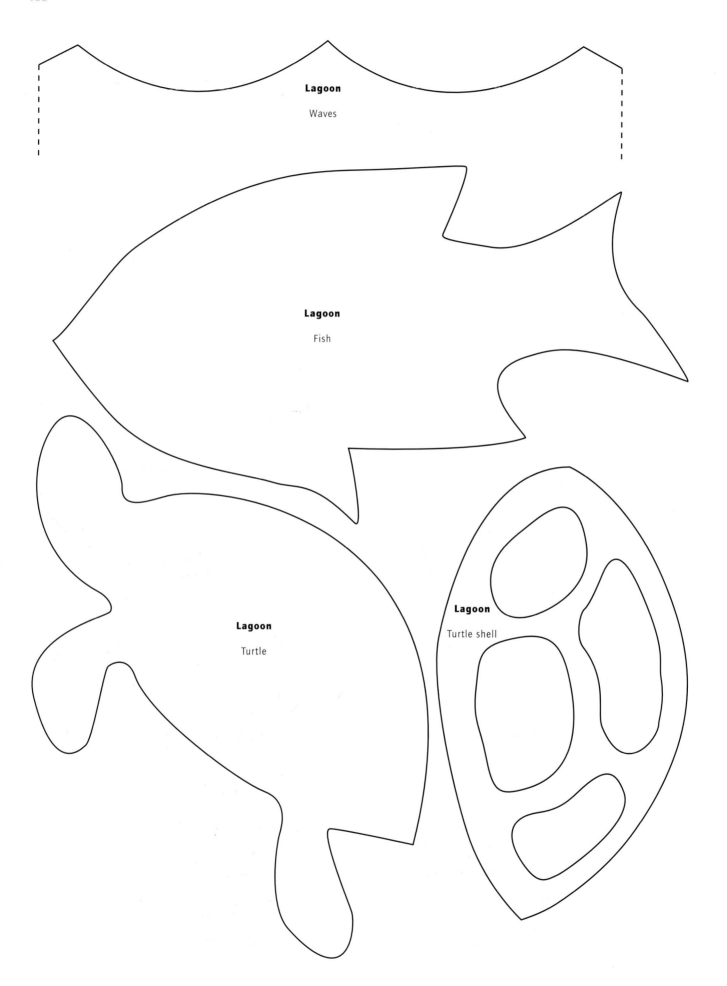

Lagoon

Waves

Lagoon

Fish

Lagoon

Turtle

Lagoon

Turtle shell

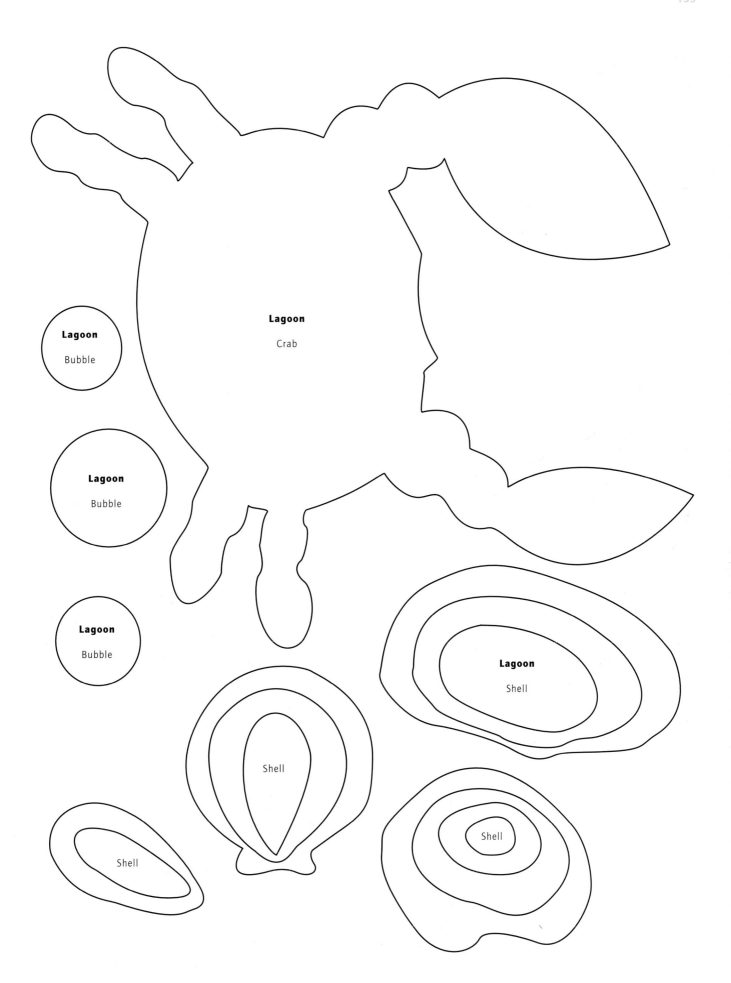

Lagoon

Crab

Lagoon

Bubble

Lagoon

Bubble

Lagoon

Bubble

Shell

Lagoon

Shell

Shell

Shell

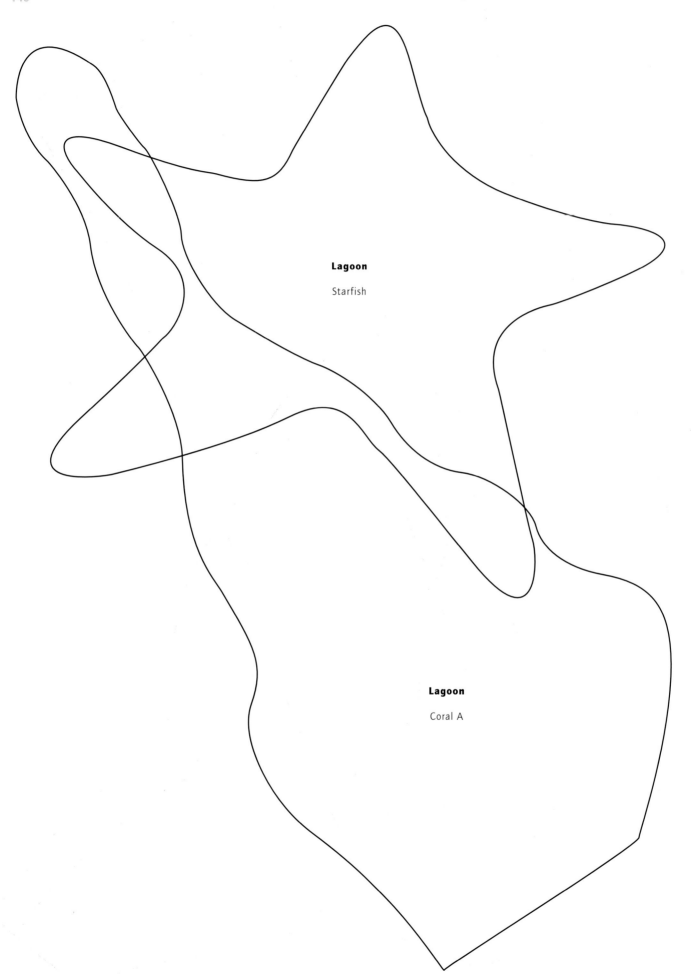

Lagoon

Starfish

Lagoon

Coral A

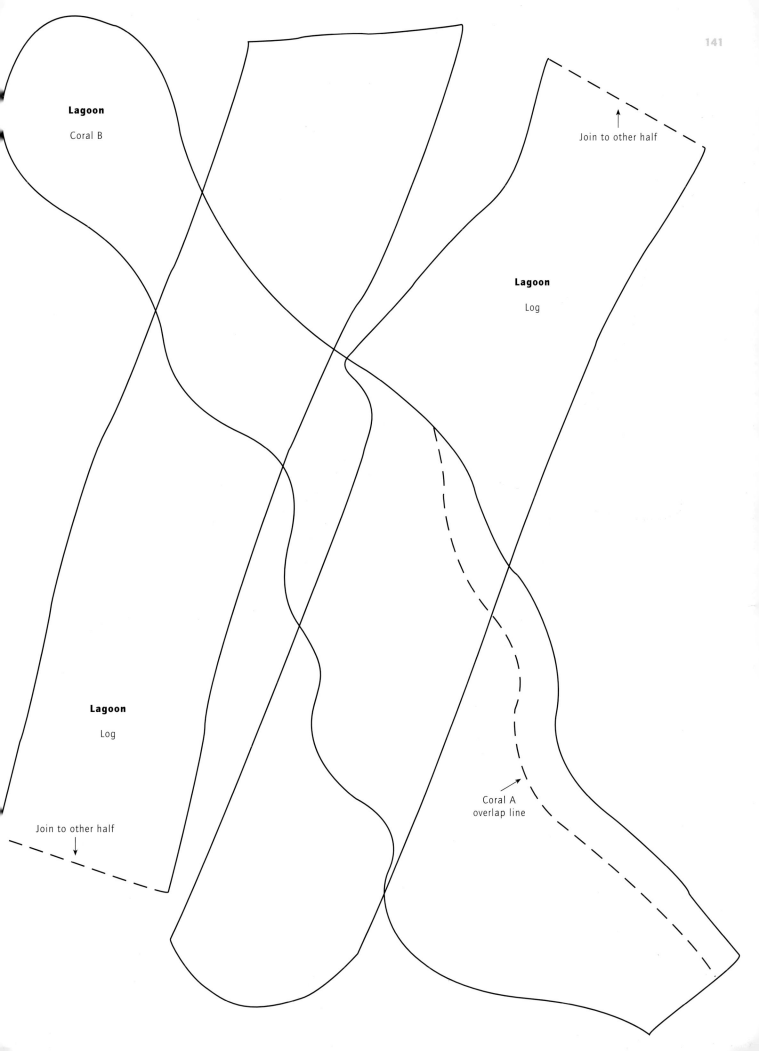

Lagoon

Coral B

Join to other half

Lagoon

Log

Lagoon

Log

Join to other half

Coral A
overlap line

Folk Flora

A: cutwork flower spray, ¼ block

Folk Flora

B: oak leaves and acorns, ¼ block

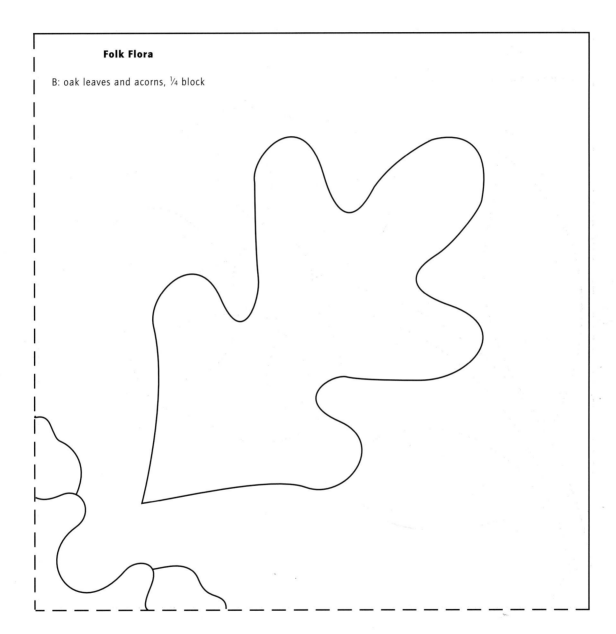

Folk Flora

C: layered cabbage rose, ¼ block

1

2

3

4

5

6